ALEJANDRO JODOROWSKY

PHILOSOPHICAL FILMMAKERS

Series editor: Costica Bradatan is Professor of Humanities at Texas Tech University, USA, and Honorary Research Professor of Philosophy at the University of Queensland, Australia. He is the author of *Dying for Ideas: The Dangerous Lives of the Philosophers* (Bloomsbury, 2015), among other books.

Films can ask big questions about human existence: what it means to be alive, to be afraid, to be moral, to be loved? The *Philosophical Filmmakers* series examines the work of influential directors, through the writing of thinkers wanting to grapple with the rocky territory where film and philosophy touch borders.

Each book involves a philosopher engaging with an individual filmmaker's work, revealing how it has inspired the author's own philosophical perspectives and how critical engagement with those films can expand our intellectual horizons.

Other titles in the series:

Eric Rohmer, Vittorio Hösle

Werner Herzog, Richard Eldridge

Terrence Malick, Robert Sinnerbrink

Kenneth Lonergan, Todd May

Shyam Benegal, Samir Chopra

Douglas Sirk, Robert B. Pippin

Lucasfilm, Cyrus R. K. Patell

Christopher Nolan, Robbie B. H. Goh

Alfred Hitchcock, Mark William Roche

Luchino Visconti, Joan Ramon Resina

Theo Angelopoulos, Vrasidas Karalis

Other titles forthcoming:

Leni Riefenstahl, Jakob Lothe

Jane Campion, Bernadette Wegenstein

István Szabó, Susan Rubin Suleiman

ALEJANDRO JODOROWSKY

Filmmaker and Philosopher

WILLIAM EGGINTON

BLOOMSBURY ACADEMIC
LONDON • NEW YORK • OXFORD • NEW DELHI • SYDNEY

BLOOMSBURY ACADEMIC
Bloomsbury Publishing Plc
50 Bedford Square, London, WC1B 3DP, UK
1385 Broadway, New York, NY 10018, USA
29 Earlsfort Terrace, Dublin 2, Ireland

BLOOMSBURY, BLOOMSBURY ACADEMIC and the Diana logo
are trademarks of Bloomsbury Publishing Plc

First published in Great Britain 2024

Copyright © William Egginton, 2024

William Egginton has asserted his right under the Copyright,
Designs and Patents Act, 1988, to be identified as Author of this work.

For legal purposes the Acknowledgments on p. vi constitute an
extension of this copyright page.

Cover image: Chilean-French filmmaker and artist Alejandro Jodorowsky
talks with Mexican vedette and actress of Argentinian origin Thelma Tixou
(1944–2019) before filming a scene during the 1989 drama film
Santa Sangre circa September, 1988 in Mexico City, Mexico.
(Photo © Bill Nation / Sygma via Getty Images)

All rights reserved. No part of this publication may be reproduced or transmitted
in any form or by any means, electronic or mechanical, including photocopying,
recording, or any information storage or retrieval system, without prior
permission in writing from the publishers.

Bloomsbury Publishing Plc does not have any control over, or responsibility for,
any third-party websites referred to or in this book. All internet addresses given
in this book were correct at the time of going to press. The author and publisher
regret any inconvenience caused if addresses have changed or sites have
ceased to exist, but can accept no responsibility for any such changes.

A catalogue record for this book is available from the British Library.

A catalog record for this book is available from the Library of Congress.

ISBN:	HB:	978-1-3501-4476-7
	PB:	978-1-3501-4477-4
	ePDF:	978-1-3501-4478-1
	eBook:	978-1-3501-4479-8

Series: Philosophical Filmmakers

Typeset by Integra Software Services Pvt. Ltd.
Printed and bound in Great Britain

To find out more about our authors and books visit www.bloomsbury.com
and sign up for our newsletters.

CONTENTS

Acknowledgments vi

1 Introduction 1

2 The Violence of Desire 11

3 Staging the Fantasy 77

4 Subjective Destitution 131

Notes 165
Bibliography 171
Index 175

ACKNOWLEDGMENTS

I am grateful to Costica Bradatan for inviting me to contribute this book to the Philosophical Filmmakers Series, and to the editorial team at Bloomsbury, especially Liza Thompson and Katrina Calsado, for their expert work in bringing it to fruition. I also want to thank several classfuls of students at Johns Hopkins for watching Jodorowsky's films with me and contributing so enthusiastically to vibrant discussions of what they mean. Of the many friends and colleagues who have discussed these ideas with me over the years, special thanks are owed to Marshall Meyers, Brooke Maddux, and Daniel Buccino, all of whom read the manuscript in its entirety and gave me invaluable feedback from deeply informed clinical perspectives. Finally, thanks are owed to Alejandro himself, who as of this writing is ninety-three years old and, not to be deterred by a little thing like advanced age, getting started on his next film.

1

Introduction

Alejandro Jodorowsky did not set out to be a therapist. The young man from the northern deserts of Chile left home for France with dreams of poetry and theater in his head. He studied puppetry and mime. He founded a radical theater group caught up in the disruptive spirit of the 1960s. They stripped off their clothes; they splashed blood; they produced actions intended to shock out of their bourgeois complacency bourgeois audiences who wished to be shocked out of their bourgeois complacency. He then started writing and directed films. In the end he only made a handful that were truly his own, but they have left an indelible impact.

His second film, *El Topo*, became a cult classic. In fact, it helped define the very notion of a cult classic. Bizarre, inscrutable, and filled with eviscerating flashes of violence and reveling in disabled and disfigured bodies, *El Topo* caught the attention of cultural luminaries like John Lennon and Yoko Ono in New York when it showed at midnight at the Elgin theater in Chelsea. The Elgin's owner Ben Barenholtz had been looking for something new to fit the changing moods of the late 60s and found it in Jodorowsky's film, which drew lines that stretched around the block night after night, and whose success fed a line of experimental shock-masters to follow, including Johns Waters, David Lynch, and George Romero.[1]

For Jodorowsky that success meant more financing for his next film. Underwritten by the Beatles' manager Allen Klein, *The Holy Mountain* made a splash at Cannes; in the United States it scored high among the stoner set. Still, for years it would be unavailable to the general public. Jodorowsky followed that up with a famous and ill-fated attempt to film Frank Herbert's epic science-fiction novel *Dune* and then a children's film about a boy and an elephant that, while it was made, was atypical in every way for him and failed to garner any distribution. In the 1980s, he returned to form with a Hitchcock-inspired psychedelic slasher film, *Santa Sangre*, followed in short order by a film he didn't write, starring Peter O'Toole and Omar Sharif, whose producer threatened to fire him if he changed a word of the screenplay. Finally in 2013 and 2016 two new films appeared, each created entirely by him: *The Dance of Reality* and *Endless Poetry*, together telling the story of his life in a creative blast of surrealist autobiography.

It was during this trajectory that, around 1980, Jodorowsky decided to apply his ideas to curing people. He started with Tarot readings— not, as he specifies, to tell the future, but to read people's present and past. In other words, he used the Tarot deck, which he had long studied and been fascinated with (and had even spent years trying to reconstruct the original Tarot deck used for occult practices, the Tarot de Marseilles) as an interpretive aid. These eventually morphed into the practice he calls psychomagic, therapeutic interventions in the form of scenarios created by Jodorowsky based on detailed interviews with his subjects and acted out by them with the help of Jodorowsky and his helpers.

INTRODUCTION 3

In 2019, Jodorowsky wrote and directed a documentary film intended to explain and clarify his psychomagic practice. He begins the film by contrasting psychomagic to psychoanalysis. The latter, he says, "was created by Sigmund Freud … its roots are scientific," unlike the former, which "was created by Alejandro Jodorowsky, a filmmaker and theater director, its roots are artistic."[2] Psychoanalysis, he goes on to claim, uses words and prohibits touching the patient, whereas psychomagic uses acts and recommends touching those who come to consult with it. His conclusion is thus quite clear: nothing could differ more than these two therapeutic practices.

And yet, here the guru errs. He errs simply because his knowledge of psychoanalysis is too popular and too limited. He betrays this attitude when he later in his film derides psychoanalysis as taking years to deliver to the patient an interpretation, "you're in love with your mother," but then leaves him or her with the question of what to do about it—unlike in his own practice, which he purports to last only a matter of hours and to deliver immediate effects. Jodorowsky's focus on the speed of his intervention recalls some of Freud's earliest thinking from the 1890s, when he experimented with hypnosis, among other fast-acting therapies, in an attempt to expedite analysis. What he found was that hypnosis was indeed capable of helping people control their symptoms, but because it didn't require the patients to experience any transference with the therapist, the relief it provided was usually short-lived, and patients ended up returning to old habits not long after the treatment ended. If Freud were alive today, he might say that psychomagic doesn't sink its teeth in deep enough to bring about lasting changes in people's psychic economies.[3]

As I argue in this book, psychomagic as well as Jodorowsky's variegated artistic production rely on interpretive practices bearing structural similarities to those of at least one brand of psychoanalysis, that of French psychoanalyst Jacques Lacan. In the three sections that follow, I lay out how Jodorowsky's art and therapeutic practice jibe remarkably closely with Lacan's theories: specifically, the dialectical nature of desire, the fundamental fantasy revealed by transference, and subjective destitution as a necessary step toward liberation.

In what ways, then, does the filmic trajectory of Jodorowsky resemble or even deploy similar mechanisms to the psychoanalytic cure as described by Lacan? To begin with, the surrealist landscapes of Jodorowsky's films as well as his therapeutic interventions recognize something fundamental about the nature of human desire: that it is dialectical, paradoxical, and self-destructive. For Lacan, who came of age as a fellow traveler of the Parisian surrealists and recognized certain truths in their art, the human animal finds in the language it uses to navigate its world both a marvelous adaptive tool and a scourge that rends the very flesh of that world—finds, in other words, the Pharmakon that was both medicine and poison in Plato's myth of the invention of writing, or "the hair of the dog that bit you," in Slavoj Žižek's more playful reference to an alcoholic's go-to hangover remedy.[4]

To put it another way, the signifier, by staying the same while referencing something different, opens a hole in the heart of human being, a clearing in the density of saturated existence that both enlightens and conceals, all the while initiating a seismic sliding toward the impression left in its wake. The most profound, the most existential of these initial mortifications are the loss of the mother's

INTRODUCTION

body, the scission of human being by sex, and the mystery of death—foundational borders of existence and identity that will ramify into a crystalline latticework of distinctions as the living being evolves.[5] For every elucidating rupture, for every internal dissociation that creates an object to reject, know, or love, unconscious traces are deposited in the form of the fantasies that form the landscape of our imaginary—solitary, incommunicable. And yet, living in the social, we are driven to share that reality via the very language that left ours in ruin. And so, language knits back together the tattered tapestry its onset left behind.

The gift of Jodorowsky, in plain sight in his earliest film and writ large in his trajectory as filmmaker, is to explore those tatters of the imaginary in all their traumatic, violent glory, while at the same time gesturing to the larger libidinal drift underlying such fragmentation. Typically, Jodorowsky frames his approach, at least in the context of his therapeutic treatments, as a break from a given tradition, in this case that of surrealism. As he puts it in his documentary, "Dalí said he wanted to bring dreams into reality. I wanted to follow the anti-surrealist path, to do the opposite. We can't teach the unconscious to speak the language of reality. We have to teach reason to speak the language of dreams."[6] But whether in the hands of surrealist painters like Dalí or a filmmaker like Jodorowsky, or through a therapeutic practice like psychoanalysis or psychomagic, reality is exposed as an imaginary landscape riddled with contradictions and violent urges, and life's journeys, as pathetic and unmotivated as they may seem, suffer from a common structure and often common sets of failures. Art, both its production and its interpretation, can be therapeutic when it involves a confrontation with the fantasies of coherence

6   ALEJANDRO JODOROWSKY: FILMMAKER AND PHILOSOPHER

that we use to escape a reckoning with the frailty, contingency, and ultimately with the inexplicability of our existence. The common arc of Jodorowsky's films manages to relate both poles of this experience: the failures that erupt—whether in the imaginary, as symptoms and causes of fear, anxiety, and suffering; or in the real, as hallucinations, delusions, or world-crushing depressions—inherently hinge on a fundamental fantasy of plenitude and redemption that is constitutively negated by the very nature of human being.

The second point of contact between Lacan's thought and Jodorowsky's art and practice, and the focus of this book's middle section, lies in the notion of transference, through which the fundamental fantasy with all its contradictions is played out on the surface. In Lacanian psychoanalysis, it is only by staging a subject's fundamental fantasies, whether in the engagement with surrealist art or in psychoanalytic practice, that the possibilities of liberation from enchainment to the ego can be realized. As the character of young Alejandro tells his friend the poet Enrique Lihn in Jodorowsky's last film, *Endless Poetry*, "you aren't suffering. What is suffering is the image you have made of yourself."[7] For liberation to take place, there must be transference. In the transference the analysand spells out in a series of stories or vignettes the arc of his or life, the peculiar pitfalls and secrets that may have led to the blockage, the repetition compulsion, now causing the subject to suffer. In this dynamic, the role of the analyst is decisive. While he or she in fact knows nothing about the analysand's secrets, the ultimate meaning tying it all together, the transference begins to take shape when the "analyst appears in the guise of the subject-supposed-to-know—to know the truth about the analysand's desire."[8]

INTRODUCTION

From the subject's perspective, the question of another who knows the shape of my desire is essentially an epistemological problem, one Lacan noted as common to science and philosophy: "Does Descartes, then, remain caught, as everyone up to him did, on the need to guarantee all scientific research on the fact that actual science exists somewhere, in an existing being, called God?—that is to say, on the fact that God is supposed to know?"[9] The truth of my desire is out there; some Other is aware of it, can work it out with enough time, given enough details; and this "subject-supposed-to-know, in analysis, is the analyst."[10] When the analysand accepts the analyst's position in this dynamic, transference is in full bloom.[11]

Guru figures and teachers who seem to know a secret or offer a secret way abound in Jodorowsky's films. Indeed, all of them include some decisive moment in which a protagonist encounters the subject-supposed-to-know and enters into something like transference. Moreover, the structural effects of transference are easily identifiable in Jodorowsky's explanation of his psychomagical practice, as well as in specific examples of the actions he designed to cure specific psychical illnesses.

Once transference has taken place and the fundamental fantasy has revealed itself, the power of the analytic discourse kicks in. As the book's third section explores, the transformative dimension of analysis comes not from the illusion of the transference itself but from the dis-illusion that takes places when the subject comes to the realization that the analyst and the trust the analysand has deposited in that role are an empty support, a kind of heuristic replacement. At this point, "this 'epistemological' incapacity shifts into 'ontological' *impossibility*; the analysand has to experience how the big Other does not possess the truth about his desire either, how his desire is without guarantee, groundless, authorized only in itself."[12] Where Jodorowsky dismisses analysis by implying that one comes to a certain knowledge, "oh, I'm in love with my mother," but then does nothing about it, in fact a successful Lacanian intervention absolutely requires going beyond such a merely passive interpretation of the symptom. It requires the step of actively identifying with one's symptom and passing through the fantasy, replacing the irresolvable dialectic of desire—its projection of impossible wholeness and satisfaction—with a recognition and acceptance of the existential fact of our finitude, our constitutive partiality and the drives it engenders.

Yet again we see precisely this kind of move in Jodorowsky's films as well as some gesture toward it in his psychomagical actions. Take the case of the desperately depressed man with frequent suicidal ideation who, in an opening interview with Jodorowsky, relates his symptoms to his deep hatred and resentment of a father who abused and neglected him. Jodorowsky brings the man to a peaceful plateau in the countryside around El Escorial, in Spain. There he performs a shamanistic surgery on the man's torso, removing his "entrails" in the form of handfuls of gooey licorice strands, before having him lie down in a grave and covering his body with dirt, leaving his head free to see and breathe under a clear bowl with holes punctured in it. He then covers the man's "grave" with carrion, thus inviting a wake of vultures that, from the man's perspective, seem to be feeding on his corpse. After removing him from the grave, Jodorowsky has the man strip naked, washes his body with milk, and then gives him a photograph of his father. The man attaches the photograph to a balloon and sends it away into the Spanish sky. In an interview taken some time after

INTRODUCTION

the action, the man reports having banished his suicidal thoughts and feeling hopeful. Specifically, he evinces a desire to love, and to be loved in return. Crucially, he makes the following point. Nothing about that love needs to be permanent. As he puts it, "If it doesn't endure that's okay. It's like life. Nothing lasts, you need to seize it."[13]

In what follows I don't expend any time arguing for the efficacity of either psychoanalysis or psychomagic. That both have convinced sufferers and garnered adherents is a simple fact. That any power they have to heal might be "just in the head" of those adherents doesn't seem to be a bug so much as a feature of each. Instead, what I try to do is show that Jodorowsky's films and therapeutic practice are guided by a coherent vision of existence, suffering, and the role art can have in providing some insight, and some relief. In this they share profound similarities with Lacanian analysis. The point, then, is not to use Lacan to explain Jodorowsky—as if one of the twentieth century's most famously obscure thinkers could make anything clearer. Rather, it is to allow an understanding of one to inform an understanding of the other, and to show what it is about both, and about human nature, that enables the effects they claim.

2

The Violence of Desire

Jodorowsky's films, like the artwork of the surrealist milieu that nurtured him, teem with fragmented bodies. Indeed, in some ways the proliferation of severed arms, castrated testicles, and deformed bodies are only the most visceral manifestation of a vast landscape of visual incoherence and audial dissonance that permeates his films. In his first film, *Fando y Lis*, the male protagonist's quest as he pushes his disabled lover's body up a hill in a makeshift cart takes the two through the rubble of a reality in ruins. A musician plays a piano that blazes amid a junkyard of detritus. The soundtrack shimmers with a detached droning akin to swarms of angry hornets—an audible signature so recurrent in the auteur's cinematic work we might venture to call it Jodorowsky buzzing. In his breakthrough psychedelic western *El Topo*, the gunslinger must fight four antagonists, each of whom has a power to alter lived reality in some fundamental way. The outcome of each duel is a bloody preview of the paroxysms that wrack the film's denouement.

In his third film, *The Holy Mountain*, a phantasmagoria of visual incoherence, a military leader builds an army of young recruits who willingly sacrifice their testicles to him. After severing them in an initiation ritual he proudly adds them as trophies to a display on his wall. In *Santa Sangre*, Jodorowsky's surrealist tribute to Alfred Hitchcock's *Psycho*, the protagonist watches as his knife-throwing father severs the arms from his religious fanatic mother—revenge for throwing acid on his groin, in turn revenge for his infidelities with their circus's tattooed lady—before slitting his own throat. The list could go on indefinitely; this is but a brief selection of examples from a few films. And yet, far from a random splatter of violent images, Jodorowsky's recurrent rehearsal of fragmentation is motivated by a singular and highly coherent philosophical vision.

This vision begins to emerge from the first lines of *Fando y Lis*. Based on the 1958 play by Spanish playwright and co-founder with Jodorowsky of the radical theater troupe Panic, Fernando Arrabal, and written together with him, *Fando y Lis* portrays the quest of the eponymous protagonists to find the mythic city of Tar. After opening with an image of Lis lying on her side and slowly eating a flower, a voiceover during the credit sequence recounts the legend of Tar, the sole city left from a mythical time before "the final war" had broken out. The voiceover speaks in second person, telling the listener that when "you" arrive in Tar, all differentiation will cease, "you will know eternity ... you will be cat, and phoenix, and swan, and elephant, and child, and old man, and you will be alone and accompanied, and you will love and be loved, and you will be here and there ... " At the end of this list the voice concludes, "you will feel ecstasy possess you and it will never abandon you."[1]

The desire of the protagonists to reach Tar is a manifestation of what we could call a drive to transcend particularity, the limitations of location in space and time, and the borders of a given identity.

THE VIOLENCE OF DESIRE

Such a desire found its most compelling expression in the work of the great Neo-Platonist and Christian theologian, Saint Augustine, when he wrote of his life that it is a "distension in several directions," and declared himself "scattered in times whose order" he could not understand. Faced with such scattering between here and there, now and then, and "storms of incoherent events" that tear at the entrails of his soul, Augustine yearned for "that day when, purified and molten by the fire of [God's] love, I flow together to merge into you."[2] While Augustine's version was religious and explicitly Christian, the problem of the One and its fragmentation into the many finds its origin in pre-Socratic thought, specifically Parmenides, and was ultimately codified by Plato, perhaps most famously in his dialogue *The Symposium*. There we are introduced in almost comic form to the myth of a prior plenitude to which humans strive by one of Socrates's interlocutors, Aristophanes, who tells the story of primordial spherical beings whose pride and power led them to threaten the gods. In response Zeus split them in half, and since that moment each broken half desperately seeks to reunite with its lost partner. This, Plato writes, is love, "born into every human being; it calls back the halves of our original nature together; it tries to make one out of two and heal the wound of human nature."[3]

The ancient myth of the human being's dissection and loss of a prior plenitude became the philosophical matrix for Jacques Lacan's understanding of how humans are alienated by language and meaning. Since outlining the understanding will be essential to the interpretation I am advancing of Jodorworsky's work, it makes sense to take a somewhat extended detour here into the Lacanian theory of the relation between language and subjectivity. From his earliest teachings and writings, Lacan associated the human loss of and desire for the recuperation of plenitude with our linguistic being. In one of his most famous and influential early articles, "The Mirror Stage as Formative of the I as Revealed in Psychoanalysis," he discusses how, during the period in which children start to acquire language, the assumption of a sense of self produces an alienation of one's embodied experience, an externalization through a mirror image of the self that is also always a misrecognition. According to the essay, the experience of perceiving him or herself in the mirror creates an imaginary sense of wholeness, and hence installs in the child's psyche an alienation essential to developing a sense of selfhood. This imaginary but crucial sense of self is then symbolically grounded by the confirmation of the experience of "reality" by a nominating third party, usually the mother or her substitute. This alienated but whole and coherent image of the self is superimposed over an experience of the body that is fragmented, contingent, and fundamentally incoherent; and indeed the self-composed out of this wreckage will always retain unconscious traces of that fragmentation—fixations, fetiches, and partial objects that will continue to organize the subject's desire later in life. But behind or beyond such local fragmentation remains the myth of redemption, of a wholeness, an ecstatic union that will heal one's original wounds. Such a mystical melding with the infinite is strictly impossible, a contradiction of the very temporal and spatial conditions of human knowledge; and thus the place of that full enjoyment is held from early on in the form of a primordial signifier issued by that nominating third party, a signifier grounded in the authority of some ultimate Other who has access to what we cannot.

The problem then becomes how the human subject's drive toward an original, illusory wholeness manifests itself or is interpreted within the context of social relations, and how the signifier of its own displacement from such full enjoyment is situated. At the individual as well as the societal level, the repeated failures to achieve a lasting, eternal peace, to permanently heal the wounds of dislocation for the individual or the antagonisms that are constitutive of social bodies, may be interpreted as temporary setbacks in the case of neuroses, or intentional blockages in the case of paranoid delusions—the work of some foreign agent or adversarial other whose presence serves to deprive us of the hoped-for satisfaction.

Blocked from achieving satisfaction, subjects deposit the key to their fulfillment in a hidden object, Lacan's *objet petit a*, that one missing thing that will certainly solve all my problems. Social groups may see the solution to achieving an elusive coherence and success as a nation, for instance, in the exclusion, suppression, or even eradication of supposed agents of harm, or in taking the object away from another subject or group that one imagines possesses it. Severe maladaptation can assume the structure of psychosis, paranoid delusions, and hallucinations in an individual, or the kind of enrapturement to totalitarian control I've elsewhere called the psychosis of power.[4] Successful adaptation, the goal of therapeutic interventions or *Ideologiekritik*, requires integrating the impossibility of a final redemption into the psychic structure, accepting the openness of the anchoring signifiers, and ultimately "passing through" the social fantasy that sustains an image of attainable fruition, coming to identify one's sense of self not with that image but with the very lacks and failures and contingencies our symptoms are meant to avoid.

Lacan came to his own as a theorist and clinician under the influence of structural linguistics, on the one hand, and the surrealist movement, on the other. While linguistics influenced his idea of how the unconscious is structured—specifically as a complex of elements relating to one another through the operations of metonymy and metaphor, with meaning being sought along a sliding chain of signification anchored by special signifiers that stand in for or hold the place of an absent, ineffable whole—the surrealists provided a model for an underlying wild and incoherent imaginary landscape that always threatens to erupt, disrupting the temporary illusions of stability provided by a symbolic détente. For Lacan the surrealist proliferation of dreamscapes and liberation of the play of signifiers was a stark reminder in the cultural world of the sea of psychosis on which sail our fragile crafts of reason. If Goya had famously warned that the sleep of reason engenders monsters, Lacan's much-touted return to Freud emphasized how reason's over-confidence had its own monstrous side.

In Lacan's system, then, signifiers giveth and signifiers taketh away. By staying minimally the same in the flux of impressions creating our lived reality, words provide the very pivot on which the perception of a self in time can turn, the very basis for what Kant called the sensible manifold to coalesce into something like coherent experience. The very same words, however, mortify us by partitioning lived experience: union with the mother's body is replaced first by a cry, then a word, and then a prohibition—a series progressively installing a phantom object calling to us from behind the receding image of a nourishing breast. Gradually a name is assumed, an identity normatively including a gender, and simultaneously implying one that one isn't. Such "gendering" through language is the theme of Lacan's famous invocation of a scene on a train recounted from the diverging perspectives of two children, a brother and a sister. As the train pulls up to the station, the boy looks out and says "look, we're at Ladies!" to which his sister replies, "Imbecile! Don't you see we're at Gentlemen?"

The point of his vignette is to undermine the classical structuralist model of signification whereby a signifier is related to an image; here, the signifiers "Ladies" and "Gentlemen" relate to otherwise identical bathroom doors, and the users' identification with the signifier relies on a certain change of assignation—depending on where they sit at a moment of assignment—in what Althusser will later call interpellation. From that moment on those terms "will henceforth be two homelands toward which each of their souls will take flight on divergent wings, and regarding which it will be all the more impossible for them to reach an agreement."[5] Impossible because, that is, to bring those wings to earth, to land them on some firm and immobile ground, would be to ground meaning and identity on something it ultimately cannot be: self-contained, self-present being, referring to no other thing than itself.

In the absence of such a landing place, the sliding of one signifier to the other, driven by the capacity language gives us to "use it to signify *something altogether different* from what it says," comes to intermittent and often arbitrary stopping points that momentarily anchor the flow and retroactively produce meaning. Here Lacan credits precisely surrealism, and its recognition that "any conjunction of two signifiers could just as easily constitute a metaphor"—as noted by its prophet André Breton, who cited as an utmost example of poetic beauty Lautréamont's invocation of "the random encounter between an umbrella and a sewing-machine upon a dissecting-table"—before adding the caveat that what really provides metaphor's creative spark is not so much the conjunction of images as the replacement of one signifier by another in the signifying chain.[6]

Lacan's innovation came from approaching something Freud had witnessed and applied to child development with the tools of structural linguistics he had learned from Ferdinand de Saussure and Émile Benveniste. Freud had described a game he saw his young grandson play with a spool and some thread, in which the boy rolled the spool out of sight and would then pull the thread until it appeared again, and then repeat the action. Whenever the spool, his toy, disappeared from sight, the boy would express dismay and utter a sound that Freud interpreted as the German word "*fort*," meaning "gone." When he pulled on the thread and his toy reappeared, he would brighten up and exclaim "*da*," here.[7]

Freud uses his anecdote to think through the issue of why humans pursue actions that clearly produce displeasure, at least at first—the child in this case purposely rolls the spool out of sight clearly knowing he will lose sight of it for a time. Lacan for his part focuses on the proto-words themselves, the alternation of a pair of signifiers on the fulcrum of the presence and absence of an object. For Lacan, it is the signifier itself that engenders the spool as a beloved object by creating the very condition of possibility for the suspension in time that allows it to vanish from sight and still exist as desired. At the junction between the sounds *fort* and *da* emerges the idea of an object that is present as absent, a kind of negative impression in the subject's world that the subject will try to fill with other objects, experiences, or relationships, but which cannot be filled by any one of them because it doesn't correspond to any one thing but is the cost extracted for the subject's very ability to use words—material entities (be they packets of sound or lines on a page) whose special gift is to always mean something other than what they are.

As the subject accumulates words and experiences, this power of the signifier expresses itself in two primary ways. First, words associate with other words by proximity, by their tendency to be used diachronically in a certain order, one leading to another. As we produce or listen to a sentence, the mind runs ahead, and certain words make sense as they fall into place. Borrowing from Benveniste, Lacan calls this movement metonymy and aligns it along the syntagmatic axis of language to describe the way in which, in our mind, one word leads to another. Second, there exists a kind of virtual plane of possible words corresponding in magnitude to the sophistication of the speaker's vocabulary that accompanies a speaker at any point in time, and that offers options to insert into the syntagmatic chain. One can conceive of this plane as consisting of more obvious, less questionable choices, the closer one is to the center, and becoming more bizarre and unexpected the further away from that point one goes.

With these tools, making sense of the world takes place across a spectrum ranging between a pole representing rote repetition and total expectation, on the one hand, and a radical innovation that correspondingly resists interpretation, on the other. Whenever we use language in its most normal, functional, everyday way—"pass me the bread, please"—the flow of language follows its diachronic axis along an expected path; the listener slightly anticipates signifiers, registers that they came as expected, and reacts in the according ways—"here you are!"; or "sorry, we're out of bread." The exchange, to use the terminology of speech act theory, is felicitous.

But even in such bland, functional contexts, the other axis of signification is at work. I could have been asking you to pass the salt; I could have ended the request with an expletive, thus radically changing the affective dimension of the exchange (like the character Sam from the sitcom *Cheers* reacting to the waitress Diane's correction of the preposition he just dangled by repeating his annoyed rejoinder with an addition at the end, "Don't you have customers to deal with, mullet head?"[8] In fact, beneath the flow of all truly human communication lies an existential dimension that corrupts any possibility of mere repetition, of language as purely empty code. As the comic George Carlin once put it about the phrase, in one's own words, "Do you have your own words? Personally, I'm using the ones everybody else has been using."[9]

Indeed, whenever we use the *universal* system of language being used by everyone else in our linguistic community, we are also struggling to use it in a way to express a particular, pathological set of experiences. I use everyone else's words, but I do so to try to express my unique take on the world. More to the point, I use them to articulate a set of desires that emerge from my existential situation. The inherent incapacity of general terms to saturate and fulfill every specific context of expression generates the specific contours of my desires. To put it with Lacan, desire emerges from the incompatibility between my needs and the demand I utter to try to satisfy those needs. The template for this generation of objects of desire is set at the onset of language use. The human child is born and remains for a relatively long period utterly dependent on adult humans to sustain it. As inarticulate cries are replaced by first words, the needs it feels and now responds to with pleas in the form of those words overflow those pitiable expressions. As a word gets stamped as a figure against the inchoate background of an inexhaustible need, the objects of desire emerge as phantom absences, promising an abundance of satisfaction should they eventually be obtained.

Naturally for a young child, the imaginary realm from which the models for such objects are drawn tends to be highly corporeal: the mother's body, specific organs, and the breasts foremost among them. That some individuals have these and offer them, and others don't, becomes an original mystery to solve. In some etiologies, perhaps the majority in traditional societies, certainly in Freud's, the child starts to theorize on the basis of routine gender roles. The mother's body provides warmth, comfort, and satisfaction from hunger. Another person is also present but more distant. He seems to have something the mother wants and thus distracts her from her all-important role of providing for the child. Most importantly, perhaps mother doesn't have it all, as she also seems to want something. Perhaps there is another for the other, one who doesn't lack himself but has the power to withhold.

As the mother's body recedes from simply being part of the nascent self, it starts to become associated with a word that can be both present and lacking. And as the other to the mother intervenes, and apparently has something the mother wants, theories start to unfold about what that Other is and has. As children grow into their respective worlds, they unconsciously associate their evolving theories with the presumed presence or lack of sex organs. Males, the father (or whoever may step into that role) foremost among them, are associated with *having* something the other doesn't have; females, the mother foremost among them, are associated with *being* something one is without.[10] To become fully sexuated within the standards of heteronormative sexuation, boys start to identify with desiring the thing that they presume men to have; and girls start to identify with desiring to be the thing they presume men want. The term Lacan then used for this thing was, of course, phallus. Phallus, however, is not a penis (indeed, what sense at all would it make to say that woman is a penis?); rather, it is the template for a lack the child presumes someone else to have access to.

Such theories are famously culturally specific and have been the source of complaints against the importation and perhaps ratification of patriarchal and even misogynist values by psychoanalysis. But part of Lacan's contribution was to expand the scope and generality of the claims, to see Freud's Victorian-tinged observations as examples of dynamics that might have a universal valence. For Lacan, gender roles may take their cue from anatomy but are in no way destined by it. They owe to situation and identification more than biology; they help structure our desires but don't determine them; far more than ultimate answers, they are placeholders for an existential question with no single answer that completely fulfills it: what am I? I am a thing in the world, made of blood and guts and cells and atoms, yes. But I also am a thing that asks itself about its origins, its existence. Am I then principally something that thinks and decides, an essence that transcends its material conditions? Perhaps in response to some scenarios; but then I always find myself in situations, constrained in time and place, and find that I am not free, but seem again more like a thing caught in the flow of a material world. I am certainly something that wants. But what decides my desires? Are they merely biological urges? Does my upbringing in a time and place have an outsize say in what I think is purely an individual will? Or do I have access to an underlying compass that can guide my decisions according to the universal laws of reason?

Lacan believed that all such questions and theories were partial expressions of the fundamental existential question of identity planted in us as children at the moment of separation from the mother's body and the implantation of language as our fundamental tool for survival. Like Kant he believed that any theory that sought to answer such an existential conundrum in its totality would produce an antinomy, a perfectly unimpeachable defense of one position ... *and* of its absolute opposing position. For example, we are utterly determined by the causal chain of the material world, *and* we are free in every moment to decide. Lacan further saw, however, that gender itself imposed an antinomic structure on our theories of the world, and ultimately on how we desire. Since a human ultimately cannot occupy all gender roles and is subject to the divisions of sexuality (something that holds for transgender and non-binary identities as well as traditional gender roles, since even identifying as non-binary and using non-binary pronouns distinguishes one from being exclusively cis-male or cis-female), individuals strive to relate what is of necessity a partial identity to a total, self-contained whole. How they do that, though, is of utmost importance to the kind of subjectivity and the structure of desire they develop.

In the patriarchal cultures that have largely dominated human history and culture, being sexuated as male involves adopting an attitude toward what Lacan calls "the phallic function" that maps precisely onto the structure of Kant's antinomies. For the male side of Lacan's graphs of sexuation, the universalization of patriarchal rules (all are subjected to the phallic function) is matched with an implicit exception (there exists one who is not subject to the phallic function)—contradictory statements that translate directly into Kant's second antinomy, which states on the one hand that everything in existence is conditioned by something else, *and* that on the other hand there exists something that is not conditioned by anything else. As per all four of the antinomies of pure reason, each side can be unimpeachably proven (or cannot be disproven) despite the same holding for its opposite. In the case of the antinomy of the conditioned or unconditioned, on the one hand, we cannot conceive of anything coming into being that is not under the influence of at least one other thing; whereas, on the other hand, in order for there to be anything at all, there must be something that conditions all of existence, and this thing cannot be conditioned by anything else. Both statements appear to be unimpeachably true, and yet each contradicts the other absolutely.[11]

Kant's solution to the antinomies was to show that they result from human reason overstepping the boundaries of its own applicability and trying to apply the laws that pertain to phenomena in time and space to the entirety of existence as it exists in itself, independent of appearances. Here Lacan borrows Kant's analysis of reason and its pitfalls to analyze something fundamental about human sexuation and its relation to desire. Specifically, it is the male side of the graphs of sexuation that exactly maps onto the antinomy. The female (or non-male) side does something different, something we might describe as approximating Kant's solution to the antinomy. For the female side of the graphs there are also two seemingly opposed statements: not all are subject to the phallic function, *and* there is no one who is excluded from the phallic function. But while the statements appear to mirror each other, it is crucial to recognize that the second one, by refusing the impulse to totalize its claim as the male side did (all are subject, everything is conditioned; there is someone who is not subjected' there exists something unconditioned), but rather constraining itself to a negative claim (not all are subject, not everything is conditioned; there is no one who is excluded' nothing is unconditioned) doesn't fall into the same trap.[12]

Indeed, by constraining itself to negations, the female side essentially adopts Kant's solution to the antinomy in that it refuses to extend the reach of its claims beyond the limits of what can be known. In this sense the negation of exceptions to the phallic function cannot be understood as a claim to have exhaustively inventoried all of humanity and positively shown that no human being exists who is not subject to wanting something he or she doesn't have access to; rather, it functions as a negation of the certainty that somewhere, out there, there exists a non-wanting, whole, and self-contained subject. Where the male and antinomic side of the graphs can only assert apodictically that all are subject to patriarchal truths (sex exists for procreation, men and women have precisely and naturally determined roles) by implicitly assuming its very opposite (that an absolutely unconditional truth, God's knowledge and will, underlies all of this and makes it so while itself remaining utterly free of any determination whatsoever), the female (or more to the point, non-male) side of the graphs merely undermines the apodictic force of the claim and, as such, squeezes by without succumbing to contradiction. In this way it resonates strongly with historicist, relativistic claims about the nature of knowledge, that by implicitly or explicitly including their own locus of enunciation in their apparently totalizing claims (as Nietzsche might have put it, everything is an interpretation, including this statement)[13] cannot be said to be self-annihilating, precisely because they negate the very logic of totality implied by the belief that a predicate must be fully consistent to be true. In other words, to hold false the statement "everything is relative" because it admits to its own relativity, is to entirely misunderstand the language of the statement. Nothing is excluded, itself included.

What does this all mean in terms of the theories a child develops as it assumes a gender and begins to organize its subjectivity and landscape of unconscious desires? To begin with let's quickly correct the term "assumes" and acknowledge that the assignment of gender is almost exclusively passive from the child's perspective. As Judith Butler has put it, the female child is "girled" though a series of language acts, ritualized behaviors, and implicit and explicit expectations, an overall process of sedimentation via what she calls, borrowing from Jacques Derrida, citationality.[14] Just as with the Carlin joke, each individual child learns to "say it in his or her own words" by using everyone else's words (and gestures, sartorial choices, etc.). And obviously the same occurs regardless of gender assignation. Indeed, children born with intersex characteristics are immediately assigned a gender at birth and often have their behavior all the more strictly controlled, precisely for fear of having the child deviate from established norms.

THE VIOLENCE OF DESIRE

One of the gendered trends that children learn—again, depending on the specific culture these can be more or less marked, more or less strictly followed, but they tend to run deeply in the vast majority of cultures—is that girls should be desired and protected, and boys should protect and desire. In other words, to become a girl in most cultures involves tacitly assuming a position whose subjective agency is always put into question, whereas to become a boy in most cultures is to assume a position whose subjective agency is emphasized. Boys are taught to desire to desire; girls are taught to desire to be desired.

We should immediately anticipate the objection that even to mention such norms critically is to implicitly ratify them, to reinscribe patriarchal values into the world as somehow natural or unavoidable. Here I join with those who find this objection not only false, but strategically problematic. Indeed, it is akin to the increasingly widespread practice on the cultural left today of believing that changing how we talk about behaviors is enough to change behaviors themselves. In fact, what more often occurs is that by pursuing such policies and policing the language of its own adherents (certainly non-adherents pay no attention whatsoever to such codes) the left merely alienates large swaths of the population and makes a mockery of its own positions. It is vile that trans people have suffered and continue to suffer the violence, hatred, and discrimination they have; but to insist that the very grammar of entire languages be changed so as not to exclude the statistically few who do not feel accommodated by the gender distinctions of, for instance, Spanish, has the perverse effect of alienating the majority of Latinos and Latinas who do strongly associate with either being Latino or Latina, and bristle at the presumption that they are somehow retrograde for not wishing to use the neologism Latinx.

As Pamela Paul has noted, this very same impulse had led to a strange trend where the cultural left seems to have joined forces with the cultural right in its traditional war on women. As she writes, for most of its history, the left saw women's rights as something to fight for. Today, in contrast, "a number of academics, uber-progressives, transgender activists, civil liberties organizations and medical organizations are working toward an opposite end: to deny women their humanity, reducing them to a mix of body parts and gender stereotypes."[15] Paul here is referring to the current trend on the part of progressive organizations to resort to circumlocution to avoid using the word "woman" in their statements about the political ramifications of decisions and policies that primarily affect, well, women. Often instead of saying that word, these organizations will use terms specific to the issue at hand, like menstruators, people with vaginas, or birthers. The high-minded intent of such verbal gymnastics, Paul concedes, is to make room for transgender and non-binary people who might retain some aspects of the traditional category of woman but not others, and who thereby might feel excluded by the more general term. But again, the outcome is the apparent rejection of an entire category of human beings and the spectacle of the first Black woman appointed to the Supreme Court being asked in her confirmation hearings to define the word "woman." We can only be thankful that the extraordinary Justice Ketanji Brown Jackson didn't feel she had to resort to the tactic of her predecessor Justice Potter Stewart, who balked at further defining hard-core pornography, in which case she might have had to say something like "I can't define a woman but I know one when I see one."

The most piquant irony is that the very move to erase woman as a self-contained category so as to remove constraints on those who might identify as women without being born that way ends up relying on the most retrograde stereotypes of femininity as criteria for those who choose that gender identification. As Paul writes again, according to the new gender theory, "girls—gay or straight—who do not self-identify as feminine are somehow not fully girls. Gender identity workbooks created by transgender advocacy groups for use in schools offer children helpful diagrams suggesting that certain styles or behaviors are 'masculine' and others 'feminine.'"[16]

It should be clear what is happening here. In their noble desire to liberate people from the constraints of traditional gender roles, advocates for the rights of trans-gender and non-binary people undermined the biological category of woman but still had to deal with the fact that many of those for whom they were trying to make space *desired to be* women. Therefore, what they *desired to be* needed to be *something*, but it needed to be something not determined in such a way that would keep them from belonging. The default position was therefore to take certain ways of behaving, dressing, and looking, which traditional societies had labeled feminine, and make *those* the standard of what makes a woman a woman rather than the exclusionary biological category. In so doing, they reified cultural categories from which the feminist movement had spent decades fighting to free women.

Paradoxically, it was with one of his most scandalous and misunderstood proclamations that Lacan essentially foresaw this

30 ALEJANDRO JODOROWSKY: FILMMAKER AND PHILOSOPHER

problematic and provided the necessary corrective. In the very seminar on female sexuality in which he sketched out the formulae of sexuation based on the structure of Kant's antinomies of pure reason, Lacan crossed out the capitalized definite article *La* before the word for woman in French, *femme*, and dared to add the declaration "La femme n'existe pas"—woman does not exist. Of course, in retrospect, the foregoing controversy reveals exactly what Lacan meant when he made this shocking pronouncement. Woman as a category can't exist because for such a category to exist it would have to be The Woman, the ideal against which all others measure themselves. The Woman doesn't exist for the very same reason that, as Wittgenstein once pointed out, the only object in the world that is neither shorter than a meter, nor longer than a meter, nor exactly a meter long, is The Meter, the gold rod kept in a temperature-maintained vault in Paris.[17] (The meter is no longer defined by that measure but is now defined by the distance light travels in a vacuum in 1/299,792,458 of a second.) In other words, what doesn't exist, as demonstrated by the current troubles around defining what a woman is, is The Woman in the sense of The Meter, the ultimate standard or point of reference that would make moot all disputes of who can be identified as women.[18]

This is why in denying the existence of The Woman Lacan was not, in fact, doing the same thing that activists are doing today when they stop using the word woman in order to make room for those who want to identify with the category. Rather, in denying the existence of an ultimate standard for defining woman (one single biological or cultural trait that would settle the debate) Lacanian psychoanalysis acknowledges that our identities aren't settled states but are always objects of desire subject to conflict and contestation. One may have requisite genitalia and be assigned a corresponding gender at birth, but this doesn't stop one from desiring to embody the cultural traits associated with the other gender; and one desires them precisely insofar as they seem always out of reach. *Or* one desires to undermine them, to assume a new identity associated with another gender. *Or* one desires to be ungendered, to be free of associations constrained by traditional social values. What almost never happens is total self-identification, total satisfaction. At which point one would cease to be a subject in almost any recognizable sense. (Admittedly, this is more or less the stated goal of many schools of Buddhism, although it is arguable whether individual monks actually achieve such states of cessation of desire.)

Indeed, the psychoanalytic critique of current positions that totally align the remains of womanhood with identity assignments that seem retrograde (women are nurturing, passive, etc.) is precisely the same as its critique of those that would exclusively assign the identity of woman to specific genitalia or chromosomes: that none of these are self-contained points of reference that settle the question and that gender identification doesn't work that way; rather, it is desire for that settled identity that always in some sense overshoots its mark, projects its object beyond whatever standard is set for it. The irony here is that it is the very logic of the patriarchal order that creates this problem. The dispute around what counts as a woman is in fact the outcome of the antinomy of sexuation produced by the male side, which insists that all are subject to the phallic function but only at the cost of projecting some One (God, The Woman) that is not thus subjected, that is whole, uncontaminated by desire, not wanting in any way. To approach the problem informed by the counter perspective—non-male, non-binary—is to glimpse the possibility of what we could call an intrinsic partiality, a not-all that doesn't require or assume the existence, somewhere, of an ultimate exception to the rule of partiality, the rule that we are always determined by desires that outstrip our control.

Thus while the female or non-male position is related to being positioned in society as an object, as one to be desired, unlike the current retrograde alignment of passivity with The Woman, what this position understands is that such positioning, when not reified into a perfect assimilation between being a woman and embodying such traits, opens onto an existential insight with the potential to liberate subjects from those social and psychological ills that can emerge from internalizing and wrestling with the pressures produced by the patriarchal identification with the universal phallic function and its excluded totality. Gender roles, and specifically identifying as female, to put it in a nutshell, neither bloom fully formed from genetic predisposition nor are they an invariable group of traits that anyone can simply opt for; rather, they cluster around an object of desire projected by culture around the signifier of The Woman. As feminist psychoanalytic theorist Juliette Mitchell once put it, seeing how deeply rooted patriarchal thinking is, and how damaging adherence to its logic can be, is requisite to achieving change.[19]

The dynamic around the loss of the mother's body, the evolving theories of sexual difference, and the unconscious influence of language come to a crest in the emergence of the *objet petit a* as the imaginary answer to what Lacan calls the dialectic of desire, pretending to resolve it by embodying the satisfaction that can't be found. As the mother's body recedes, the child learns words to articulate its needs, words that simultaneously represent the presence and lack of potential but always fleeting satisfactions. As the child's linguistic range becomes more sophisticated, he or she becomes inhabited by longer and more complex signifying chains. The chains flow along both axes, the syntagmatic and the paradigmatic, the former guiding the child's desire from concept to concept, from object to object, the latter permitting the sudden replacement of one concept with another, of one object with another. A field of meaning, of fundamental values begins to settle for the child, his or her theories and certainties guided by the metonymic flows of meaning themselves occasionally anchored by metaphors. Such metaphors take on the feeling of unimpeachable truths, incontrovertible values, in the child's ideological landscape. Freedom, God, and love—massive words that the emergent subject lives and could even die for, but words that ultimately don't and cannot bequeath meaning to his or her system because they only receive meaning retroactively from the rest of the system as a whole. They are essentially empty signifiers that, like The Woman herself, are always contested, always up for grabs.

One way to understand how these metaphors come to organize our symbolic world and identities is the Lacanian notion of "quilting points" (*points de capiton*). As Slavoj Žižek puts it in *The Sublime Object of Ideology*, "The *point de capiton* is the point through which the subject is 'sewn' to the signifier, and at the same time the point which interpellates individual into subject by addressing it with the call of a certain master-signifier ('God', 'Freedom', 'America')—in a word, it is the point of the subjectivation of the signifier's chain"[20] (112). Thus, such empty "master signifiers" emerge from the point at which a subject locates him or herself in a meaningful world, the point at which his or her very sense of self is forged in the soldering of this intrinsically meaningless master-signifier to an existing system of meaning (e.g., linking freedom to the right to carry guns, or linking it to legislation banning guns).

More complicated still, what the quilting points come to stand in for are in essence gaps in the fabric of meanings that make up our lives. As we cannot directly represent the recesses that emerge as we lose embeddedness in the physical world, we replace them with fundamental metaphors—fundamental because in this case they aren't merely replacements for other words, but replacement for an inability to account for our ultimate attachment to something. Our libidinal attachment to these nodes in our symbolic universe is powerful indeed. They account for why ideological edifices are so hard to shatter, why people are often more willing to lay down their life than give up on a particular take on the world, on religion, or on family and gender roles. The award-winning Swedish film *When Darkness Falls* by Anders Nilsson gives a particularly gruesome example of this in the story of an immigrant family in Stockholm whose patriarch, along with the other men in his family, conspires to murder his own daughter for the mere perception of her cavorting with men and hence destroying what they and their culture perceive to be the family's honor.[21] Such honor killings were the principal fare of the literary boom in Spain in the early modern period, with people flocking to the theaters each week to watch graphic depictions of how men could be compelled to murder the women they ostensibly love over the suspicion of infidelity. As I've worked out elsewhere, the reason the signifier "honor" could exert such control over people's imagination is precisely because of how it functioned as a quilting point in the early modern Spanish state's construction of national identity.[22]

Honor killings are also a good example of the dynamic at hand because of the combination of attraction and repulsive horror that animates them. While it would be easy and more than understandable to simply dismiss and condemn the character of the father in *When Darkness Falls* as a lunatic who deserves the worst punishment imaginable for the heinous and incomprehensible crime of murdering his own daughter, the film (and actor) also brilliantly portray the eviscerating anguish of his decision, as he is emotionally drawn and quartered by the love for his child and the obscene compulsion to cleanse the family's honor with her death. Indeed while such an example is as extreme as it gets, the dichotomy lurking behind such fundamental metaphors is constitutive of what Lacan called the dialectic of desire, and characterizes the *objets petit a*, the pathological objects of our desires that are situated by the organization of metaphors in our unconscious. Yes we pursue such objects, but we also fear (with good reason!) actually finding them. The ambivalence staged by Freud's grandson, the repetition of the alternation of pleasure and displeasure at the deliberate loss and rediscovery of his new toy, all of this plays out with greater and greater stakes as the child grows and his or her psychic and emotional worlds develop in complexity.

At a developmental stage quite a bit later than that of Freud's grandson, my own son showed precisely such an example of the fundamental ambivalence of desire in his relationship to a character in a Disney film, *The Lion King*. There, without any doubt, his favorite character was the villain Scar, voiced with silky malice by Jeremy Irons; but my son was also so terrified by Scar that he would run from the room whenever the villain entered the screen—only to furtively poke his head through the door and ask, voice atremble, "Scar?" As Lorenzo Chiesa has described it, the very scenario whereby a fundamental fantasy is installed as a kind of veil over the impossible lack at the heart of our psychic life does indeed have something of the nature of a horror film:

> To put it bluntly, when the child freezes the shocking scene of the film he is accidentally watching unaware of its traumatic content—when he originally organizes the unbearable encounter with the Real of the desire-of-the-(m)Other which causes anxiety—he both obtains a still that protects him from the trauma (through the imaginary objectification of the scene) *and* lets himself be partially traumatized (through the real scene which underlies its imaginary objectification). In other words, *thanks to* the mitigation of the screen/veil that "fixes" what Lacan calls "the full scene," the child ends up "enjoying" what he has seen, and wants to watch it over and over again.[23]

The virtue here of Chiesa's analogy is that it permits us to conceptualize both the horror/attraction duality of the *objet petit a* and the repetition compulsions that its inherently dialectical nature can produce. The fantasy screen is a veil that protects us from the trauma of the loss of satisfaction around which our psychic life is organized; as such it simultaneously imparts attraction toward the loss it covers over, and repulsion at the loss. Our desire pushes us to pierce that veil in the vain hopes of recovering what we have lost, but unconsciously we know that trauma lies on the other side, and we retract in horror. We thus find ourselves in a holding pattern, ceaselessly repeating the approach, only to pull back and begin once again.

And it should come as no surprise at this point to see that this pattern and the poles of the dynamic encode a particular gender logic. Namely, to be sexuated as male, to identify primarily with the one who beholds, desires, and intervenes, is to embody most fully the perverse and self-destructive dialectic of the *objet petit a*, a fact that explains why of the various patterns of neurosis that psychoanalysis identifies those of perversion and obsessive-compulsive disorder are predominantly experienced by those who identify as male. Correspondingly, those who identify as female may more often suffer from what used to be called hysteria, originally and absurdly associated with the surreal image of the wandering womb, but now referred to as functional neurological symptom disorder or conversion disorder, a term that is essentially the DSM equivalent of shrugging one's shoulders and saying, "there doesn't seem to be anything physically or neurologically wrong with you—I recommend therapy." Sufferers of this general class of disorder are characterized by emotional distress, periods of dissociation and even seizures, and physical manifestations of symptoms that don't appear to have physiological or neurological causes. From a psychoanalytic perspective, the (again, old-fashioned) term hysteric refers to suffering from an unconscious conflict that, not finding expression in conscious form, expresses itself metaphorically in the body or in some self-damaging behavior. But what really distinguishes the structure of hysteria from that of obsessive neurosis or perversion is, per Lacan, its discursive structure.

For Lacan the discourse of the hysteric entails a certain progress from the discourse of the pervert or obsessive, in that it is characterized not by the fetishistic disavowal of the lack at the heart of one's psychic organization, but rather a persistent question directed to the other as to what it desires of me, what I am to it, what, ultimately, does it want me for? Naturally this question also leads to suffering and, at a pathological level, to powerful reaction formations. But at heart the question channels an existential openness to precisely the possibility that the other positions most desperately seek to undermine or disavow, namely, that the other doesn't have an answer for you, a purpose for you, that the other is unsupported by any ultimate raison d'être.

The poles of sexuation, then, those "two homelands toward which each of their souls will take flight on divergent wings," are broadly characterized by either the tendency to desire to be like someone who *has* what the other desires and thereby grounds the law while remaining excluded from it, or to desire to be like someone who *is* what the other desires, and who also unconsciously believes that the law doesn't fully define her desires, but that no one really escapes its aegis either. As Vicky Krieps says in the role of Sisi, Empress of Austria, in Marie Kreutzer's 2022 film *Corsage*, speaking to her English lover, "I love looking at you looking at me." Her desire is to be desired, a discursive position that predisposes those who adopt it to suffer from certain symptoms, but also opens the door to potential resolutions not available to those who identify with the master of exceptions.

That the entry to language and meaning and the resulting mortification of human psychic and embodied life are imprinted by the divisions of sexuality is absolutely key to understanding Jodorowsky's films, his therapeutic praxis, and the philosophical import of both. To return to his first film, *Fando y Lis*, there the two protagonists fully take on the roles of Lacan's boy and girl arriving at the station, defining themselves as denizens of "two homelands toward which each of their souls will take flight on divergent wings, and regarding which it will be all the more impossible for them to reach an agreement." In disparate scenes and apparent flashbacks we see how Lis's memories are tinged by horrific scenes of being treated as a doll in a puppet theater as a young girl, hounded by various male characters and controlled by an eerie puppet master (played by Jodorowsky, who studied puppeteering and mime in France). As the grown counterpart to Fando, she is confined to a doll-like state, paraplegic and in need of Fando's help to move anywhere. Fando for his part fawns on Lis and tries to prove his relevance to her, pushing her on his cart and repeating the promise that all will be made whole when they finally arrive in Tar. But his attentions also erupt into abuse. He despairs of her immobility and leaves her on the ground, telling her she must crawl. At another time he appears to be trafficking her, inviting a parade of random people (evocative of the theater troupe that molested her in her memories) to admire and paw her naked body like chattel.

Time and time again violence spasms into reality when the paradoxical and hidden object/cause of desire, whose absence is required for the fabric of reality to cohere, comes too close to the surface, leading to a derealization of reality in which "reality is no longer structured by symbolic fictions; fantasies which regulate the imaginary overgrowth get a direct hold on it."[24] Here we see the perverse "logic" behind Fando's treatment of Lis, alternatively worshipping her and abusing her, promising to serve her and provide for her, and then turning around and handing her over to pawing, drooling men.

40 ALEJANDRO JODOROWSKY: FILMMAKER AND PHILOSOPHER

Indeed, what these scenes demonstrate is the truth that the famous whore/virgin divide isn't a divide at all. Rather, the misogynist fantasy is structured on the very impossibility of a woman occupying both sides of the same coin of the other's desire. For in desiring to be the ideal object of desire defined by the patriarchal order, Lis must essentially embody both sides of a self-negating contradiction—on the one hand the veil of purity, a mirror telling the man that he is the only one, that she as woman will always serve as the ultimate safeguard of his honor, holding him above all other men; and on the other the very embodiment of concupiscence, a ravenous lust that no man could ever fulfill.

In fact, in his combined hatred and desire of women the misogynist desires both sides, simultaneously, precisely *because* they are in contradiction, embodying as they do the very object-cause of his desire in all its ambivalence, that primal fantasy-*cum*-horror film that both acts as veil over the abyss of his founding lack and last possible link to the satisfaction he imagines to be found there again.[25] Naturally, though, he explodes in violence when confronted by the truth of his own fantasy, that his paragon of purity must also be a vortex of vice. Herein lies the humor of a scene like that in the 1999 comedy *Analyze This!*, in which mafia boss Paul Vitti, played by Robert De Niro, seeks help from Billy Crystal's Dr. Ben Sobel:

—What happened with your wife last night?
—I wasn't with my wife, I was with my girlfriend.
—Are you having marriage problems?
—No.
—Then why do you have a girlfriend?

—What, are you gonna start moralizing on me?

—No, I'm not, I'm just trying to understand, why do you have a girlfriend?

—I do things with her I can't do with my wife.

—Why can't you do them with your wife?

—Hey, that's the mouth she kisses my kids goodnight with! What are you, crazy?[26]

Unfortunately, this comic scene hides a far darker, more frightening truth: the millions of women brutalized and killed each year by so-called jealous partners, whose jealousy is little more than the projection of their own fantasies.

The brilliance of Jodorowsky's vision in *Fando y Lis* stems from how he allows the destructive dynamics of patriarchal desire to play out against the mythical logic of Tar, that is, of the fundamental fantasy underlying all desire: that our partiality, our lack, is temporary, ephemeral, and that we can find unification and ultimate satisfaction not just of partial, temporary desires but of Desire per se by reunifying with "the one," as in, "do you think she/he is the one, the one you've been searching for your whole life, your match made in heaven?" In this way the film dramatizes one of Lacan's most enigmatic dicta, namely, that there is no such thing as the sexual relationship, in the sense of Aristophanes's pre-existing man-woman creature, the conjoined whole we desperately seek to rejoin.

The fact that desire is also metonymic, driven relentlessly from one object to another, always in search of novelty, of course radically contradicts that former ideology. Fando both wants to see Lis as desirable for others, as desiring being desired by others, and as the

42   ALEJANDRO JODOROWSKY: FILMMAKER AND PHILOSOPHER

one, the quilting point and stoppage of the flow of desire that exists only for him. Lis for her part desires to be desired by Fando and can only be desperately confused at the contradictory models his desire holds up for her, models young women are implicitly and constantly told they should inhabit today: sexy but unattainable, slutty but pure. Indeed, our congratulatory back-patting at how far we've come taming the misogynist angels of our nature can only come a cropper every time we turn on the TV or look at any of an apparently limitless numbers of videos shared on social media, as young women desperately strive to embody the riven role thrust at them by patriarchal culture.

Fando y Lis's surrealist tincture allows it to explore the imaginary logic of such self-destructive striving to its absurdist consequences, as Fando desperately traffics his beloved only to stone her to death at the sight of her perceived infidelity to him. The result, only in his dreams: a reborn Lis, pure and white as the lily she consumes in the film's opening frames (*lis* means lily in French), rising from the grave of her martyrdom and naked as Eve in the garden before her first taste of sin, awaiting Fando, equally naked and pure, cleansed of his sins, to run together into the Eden of their love. In this sense Jodorowsky seems to be doing something akin to what Todd McGowan argued is the central move in David Lynch's groundbreaking series *Twin Peaks*, where he argues that Lynch's surrealist approach to the character of Laura Palmer and the mystery of her murder is a way of exploring the impossible and contradictory demands made upon women—to be both Madonna and whore, both loving mother and sex object. Indeed embodying those contradictory desires is such an impossible task that we hardly ever see her throughout the series, but in the follow-up film *Fire Walk with Me* we see her volunteering after school one day, then taking drugs and having sex the next. She thus exists in this impossible space that satisfies both of the mutually exclusive demands thrust upon her, the effect of which can only be surreal to whoever's watching it.[27]

Jodorowsky's next film after *Fando y Lis* was his breakthrough *El Topo,* the esoteric mashup of vaguely eastern philosophy with western gunslinging dubbed by Pauline Kael in a review in the *New Yorker* as an "acid western," in which she described the movie as participating in a counterculture in which "viewers have begun to look for the equivalent of a drug trip in its theatrical experiences."[28] *El Topo* is nothing if not trippy. The film opens with the Black-clad title character riding his horse in an unforgiving dessert with a naked little boy. The two unmount, squat down in the sand, and the gunslinger gives the child a teddy bear and a silver frame. In the first lines of the movie, the gunslinger tells the little boy "You're seven today. You're a man now. Bury your first toy and the portrait of your mother."[29] From this point on we are treated to a non-stop avalanche of surreal violence and sex, as El Topo first frees a woman from a despotic general and then proceeds, at her encouragement, to track down and confront four epic gunmen, each with special powers that have previously made them invincible.

The nature of this set-up, these confrontations, and the violence they enact is already of interest. El Topo's first words to his son in some ways embody the very function of language in the individuation of a child, asking him to replace childhood and specifically the image of his mother with the concept he should henceforth identify with, man. It is this identification with the signifier man that then seems to trigger the stream of violence, as if the effort of the film were expended on answering the question, what does it mean to become a man? In a repetitive reenactment of Hegel's master/servant dialectic, initially the answer seems to be, to become a man one must confront and overcome the one who holds the power of death over you while himself seeming to be free of that fear. The Colonel is a classic primal father in this sense. Like the iconic figures in Freud's myth of the emergence of civilization, *Totem and Taboo*, the Colonel sadistically enjoys all women while withholding that privilege from his slavish male followers or, in the case at hand, eventually serving them "his leftovers," violently pushing his lover to the ground and ordering his men, like dogs, to eat.

At this very moment El Topo enters the compound and defeats the collected men with his gunslinging skills. He then gives the Colonel a gun and challenges him to a duel. The duel is a pure humiliation for the Colonel. El Topo turns his back on him and spreads out his arms. But as the Colonel raises his gun to shoot, El Topo fires a backward shot without looking that hits him in the hand and strips him of his gun. El Topo then shoots off his hat, strips him and has his men hold him down on the ground. He then takes out his hunting knife and castrates him. The naked, bleeding man takes a few faltering steps away to a pistol lying by a stone wall, which he picks up and kills himself with.

Perhaps we could speculate that the recurrence of scenes of castration in Jodorowsky's work suggests that in some sense castration is the goal of surrealist film in general. Surrealism presents the viewer with random imagery the viewer doesn't know what to do with, imagery that doesn't push the narrative forward in any clear way, thus highlighting the viewer's sense of impotence in the face of visual incoherence. The inclusion of scenes of castration in *El Topo* and *The Holy Mountain*, as well as analogous sequences we will discuss in some of his later films, would be Jodorowsky literalizing on screen what he believes his films are doing to his viewers. Indeed, as we will explore in greater detail below, the same could also be said for his persistent inclusion of characters with physical deformities. It's not just that Jodorowsky finds all bodies beautiful, as he has put it himself, but rather that he sees in these bodies a potent metaphor for the human form in general, its impotence relative to the images with which it routinely (mis)identifies.

There can be no doubt that the invocation of Freud and the primal father is pertinent here. In Freud's myth the father's enjoyment of women and the privation of this enjoyment for his sons is the foundational struggle of civilization.[30] In Freud's telling, the primal horde eventually rises up and kills the father. The dead father then becomes deified by the tribe in the form of the totem, representing the law and fundamental prohibitions, such as the incest taboo, around which cultures are established. The totem or nascent God thus takes over the role of the exception in Lacan's formulation of sexuation— all are subject to the phallic function (the laws, limitations, and castration in the sense of privation of enjoyment) *and* there is one who is not subject to it. In Jodorowsky's version, El Topo's drive becomes that of embodying the primal horde and killing the father, even more specifically (and graphically), taking from him the symbol of his enjoyment. Tellingly, what the film also demonstrates and explores is how the unconscious belief in the exceptional status of the father implicitly drives male violence. In a perverse sense, *El Topo* is the embodiment of the fantasy that plays out in the minds of so many of the mass murderers who plague US schools, young men who have been isolated and bullied, who then dream up a world in which they are the avenging hero. As David Brooks writes about the psychology of such mass murderers,

> [T]hey craft a narrative in which they are the hero. The world is evil, and they will stand up to the world. Or the world is in catastrophic danger. The Blacks/Jews/women are destroying us, and they will strike back. These internet-fueled narratives have an arousing power. They make them feel righteous, strong and significant. People whose lives are dissolving into chaos will grasp any black-and-white story that provides order and purpose.[31]

Indeed, in this respect it is unsurprising that Jodorowsky previews by almost three decades the iconography of school shooters created by Eric Harris and Dylan Klebold when they perpetrated the atrocity now associated with the name of their town and high school, Columbine. Wearing dusters inspired by western gunslingers and, in fact, similar to the black leather attire not only of *El Topo* but also popularized by the mega blockbuster screening the very year they went on their rampage, *The Matrix*, the troubled young men mercilessly mowed down their fellow students like so many video-game zombies, drunk on the power of their arsenal.

I'm not arguing that those who flocked to the Elgin in Chelsea in 1970 to see *El Topo* were aware of any implicit critique of male violence. There Pauline Kael's analysis seems more likely, namely, that *El Topo*'s trippiness, its bizarre marriage of western violence and Zen, appealed to a public desirous of drug-fueled pseudo-profundity and general boundary-breaking. What they liked in *El Topo* was its

THE VIOLENCE OF DESIRE

excessiveness. But with anything approaching an in-depth view of the movie, it's hard to grasp the overall arc of Jodorowsky's film as anything but an interrogation of male violence and even a (failed) search for its cure.

El Topo (the character as opposed to the film) seems driven to kill by a force that exceeds his conscious awareness. He is also urged on by the desire of the woman he saves from the Colonel. Between those two influences he decides to confront the four invincible gunslingers, defeating each in turn. But if he hopes for release or absolution, each time he encounters greater distress and greater anguish.

His first encounter, with a yogi-like master who can open and close his own flesh to let bullets pass through him, occurs right after his companion has spurred him to fight, telling him that she can only love him if he shows he is the best. It is clear that her character is entirely associated with imaginary rivalry and the aggressions that ensue from it. El Topo overcomes the yogi master with trickery, leaving a hole in the sand in his path, and shooting him as he falls down into it. After winning the duel his lover exults in his success, telling him she knew he would prevail, and that there are only three masters left to defeat. As she bathes in an oasis, a new woman approaches on horseback, and then appears nude by the water's edge holding a mirror. In the water she presents the first woman with the mirror, who then begins to admire herself in it. Later, when she and El Topo have sex in the desert sand, while El Topo is consumed with desire for her, the woman clearly desires being desired, and holds a mirror up to her own face. After the act she rides on her horse, still consumed by her own image, and El Topo turns and shoots the mirror from her hand, pocketing one of its shards.

The juxtaposition between the woman's infatuation with her own image and desire to be desired, on the one hand, and El Topo's violent conflagration, on the other, couldn't be clearer. He seeks to enter into that hermetic space of her desire, to be worthy of it, and reacts with violence when he cannot. Like the boy who has been told to bury his first toy and the portrait of his mother, the gunslinger seeks to replace something irreplaceable with the desire of another. But her desire is self-focused; El Topo even watches as she and the new woman enter into a relationship of mutual desire (later they will laugh together as they fill him with gunfire). So, failing to fill that void with the desire of another, he lashes out at the very imaginary register that represents her narcissism. Like school shooters desperately lashing out at what they see as the frame (in their case the school community) that has excluded them, El Topo's anger is directed against the frame that excludes him, and only targets specific rivals when that frame (namely, the woman's desire) points him to them.

It seems important here to address a controversy that arose years after the release of *El Topo* that very much has to do with these scenes in the desert. In an interview given around the time of the release while he was promoting the film in the States, Jodorowsky said to an interviewer in reference to the actress who plays the woman, Mara Lorenzio:

> After she had hit me long enough and hard enough to tire her, I said, "Now it's my turn. Roll the cameras." And I really ... I really ... I really raped her. And she screamed. Then she told me that she had been raped before. You see, for me the character is frigid until El Topo rapes her. And she has an orgasm. That's why

I show a stone phallus in that scene … She has an orgasm. She accepts the male sex. And that's what happened to Mara in reality.[32]

After the interview was "rediscovered" in 2020 around the theatrical rerelease of *El Topo* and several screenings were cancelled in protest, Jodorowsky entirely retracted what he said in the interview. He said he did absolutely did not rape her; that he was trying to market an avant-garde film in a foreign country with no money and relied on shock values to do so. He pointed out that during that period of marketing the film he intentionally blurred the boundaries between fiction and reality and stayed in character as El Topo. He made the point that to commit such a rape and have it remain unreported years after would have been utterly impossible. To shoot such a scene he needed multiple cameras and dozens of crew members around, any of whom could have reported the crime.

Even if true, his later retractions don't excuse the obvious sexism in the statement itself, even if it was meant to express something about El Topo's character. In fact, there is a vector of Jodorowsky's belief system, evident in his writings and practice as well as his films, that clearly jibes with a vision of men having a natural role as active, even aggressive, desirers, and women as having a natural role as passive recipients of that desire. In one psychomagic cure, for instance, Jodorowsky stages a kind of spiritual rebirth for a man who was abused and bullied as a child and has suffered from a crippling stutter ever since. Part of the act involves the man stripping naked in a temple, his genitals painted red while his body is painted gold. Jodorowsky then lays hands on the man, specifically his genitals, and has him engage in primal screaming about his manhood and his virility, in essence

50 ALEJANDRO JODOROWSKY: FILMMAKER AND PHILOSOPHER

reclaiming in his lost voice the virility of his manhood as represented by the phallus.

Assuming no manipulation of the video evidence, the cure worked, for a man who couldn't utter a single sentence without being caught up in his stutter is able to give an entire exit interview some weeks after with no evident difficulties and a great deal of evident relief, even joy. The question, then, is what specifically worked in his case? Was it an issue of readapting to a patriarchal order that aligns being a man exclusively with subjective activism, with the willingness to take what one desires? On the one hand, at times Jodorowsky appears to support such a naturalist vision of human nature. On the other, however, he openly condemns homophobia and seems to have done so from a relatively early age. Indeed, one of the (from the video evidence well attended) actions he performed in public was a literalization of leaving (and destroying) the closet, and a public performance of a gay marriage. Thus it would be hard to argue that his philosophy specifically regards human essences as heterosexually determined, even if he still might associate certain subjective and desiring positions with being a man and vice versa. Indeed, given his open embrace and even obvious love and enjoyment of the non-normal, the non-conforming, it seems unlikely that Jodorowsky believes that social normativity should be defended as an ethical principle.

Rather, I think that in the very specific case of gender identities Jodorowsky adopts a more Jungian approach to sexuated positions, believing in something like an eternal masculine and eternal feminine principle. Associating manhood with learning to assert desire and womanhood with learning to accept being desired could be one logical outcome of such a gender philosophy, though certainly not one that

Lacanian psychoanalysis supports. What the latter does support and what I believe is unconsciously present in Jodorowsky, is the idea of a specifical set of blockages and social and personal disorders that are fostered by the patriarchal order, and ultimately a similar set of steps that could be helpful in freeing up those blockages. In the case of Jodorowsky's despicable statements about Mara achieving orgasm because of rape, they certainly do fit the character of El Topo, which he claims, with some credibility, to have been inhabiting at the time—a character who is stuck within the violent feedback loop of the patriarchal order. Indeed, what the diegetic narrative shows is that ultimately no liberation results from that patriarchal presupposition. El Topo sows and reaps only violence; every attempt to pass through to another level ends in failure, and bloody failure at that.

Whatever the means, with *El Topo* Jodorowsky made a commercially successful arthouse film and one that drew attention from a wide spectrum of influencers. The entrée into The Beatles's world through the admiration of John and Yoko was most likely Jodorowsky's most fortunate asset. Soon after the success of *El Topo* he gained access to funding for his third film through The Beatles's manager Alan Klein, who became its executive producer. The film, made for almost a million dollars entirely in Mexico, was *La montaña sagrada* (*The Holy Mountain*), a technicolor phantasmagoria with clear surrealist influences from Buñuel and Dalí, that has been called the "best surreal film ever" made.[33]

The Holy Mountain picks up on several of the themes Jodorowsky had explored in both his previous films. Some kind of goal, with some kind of enlightenment, is at stake, albeit this time for several main characters as opposed to one. At the outset of the film, it appears as though it will follow the mold of a central male character seeking that goal and enlightenment. In this instance that character is "the thief," a loincloth-wearing Jesus-lookalike whose Christological appearance is explicitly explored in an early scene. In that scene, the thief's body is used as a mold to create Jesus statues. We see him carry a cross like Christ; lie upside down on a pile of Jesus statues made in his image; and lasciviously eat the plaster face off one of the statues made in his image. Christological imagery wasn't new to Jodorowsky. When El Topo is shot by his two female consorts, as he staggers toward them, each of their shots opens a wound in his body that corresponds to one of Christ's stigmata. But what does Jodorowsky achieve by associating otherwise venal or even ultraviolent men with Christianity's idea of God?

The common link can be found in René Girard's idea of the scapegoat. A version of Freud's myth of the primeval horde and its murder of the father, Girard's version of what he called the scapegoat mechanism serves for him as a foundation of culture. Early cultures all engaged in scapegoating, in depositing the ills of their society onto a single entity, person, or animal that would then be ritually killed in an effort to restore an order, peace, or prosperity assumed to have been lost. For Girard these early cultures never entertained the idea of an innocent scapegoat; rather, the process of substituting some being for the cause of their troubles was an unconscious one. It was with Christianity (and this is why for Girard Christianity represented the highest religious order) that the process left the darkness of the unconscious and entered the light of conscious reflection. For in Christianity the savior embraces the role of sacrificial victim to expiate the sins of all men and does so despite his complete innocence.[34]

In this light, the transposition onto El Topo and the thief of obvious Christological imagery signifies a transition from random externally oriented violence to consciously assumed self-sacrifice. In *El Topo* the transition is clear and marks a turning point in the film. The gunslinger has defeated all four masters and still not achieved enlightenment; he is still tortured by desire. His stigmata-murder by the women leaves him a quasi-corpse, which is then carried into a cave by a group of disabled and destitute people who live there excluded from and in the shadow of the nearby "civilization," a western-style town replete with bourgeoisie, saloon, and church. From that point on he will be transformed, reborn as a monk-like pacifist, even if his attempts to be a savior for his "people" end in total failure.

In the case of the thief, his Christological moments seem to be a continuation of the death and rebirth in the previous film. The film opens with the thief lying prostrate, apparently dead or almost dead, his face covered in flies, and urine streaming from his pants. He is then discovered by a quadriplegic dwarf with a Tarot card pinned to his back. After cleaning his face, the dwarf is joined by a host of naked children who carry the thief away. In the next scene we see him suspended on a cross where he is pelted by stones thrown by the children. Rather than kill him, the stoning seems to (and have been intended to) result in the awakening of the thief, who descends from the cross and approaches his "people" as a kind of god. The "god," however, yells at the children, who scatter. He then threatens the dwarf with one of the stones. The dwarf cowers, the thief relents. They smoke a joint together and reconcile, the dwarf licking the thief on the face while the thief smiles and laughs. He then puts the dwarf on his shoulders, and they make their way into the city.

There they are surrounded immediately by scenes of extreme violence. A huge cart laden with the bloodied bodies of (presumably) the naked children passes by; Mexican soldiers shoot bound and blindfolded students; and, as if to emphasize the theme of the scapegoat, a procession passes with dozens of bloody goat or sheep carcasses splayed out on upheld crosses. The thief and his companion are quickly coopted into the touristic marketplace of modern Mexico. As tourists excitedly photograph the soldiers who have just killed the students, a soldier has sex with a female tourist while her husband pays the bemused thief to film them. He then happily barkers for one of Jodorowsky's most famous scenes, a reenactment of the conquest of Mexico with the Aztecs played by chameleons and the Spaniards by toads.

It is at this point, with the stage made in the image of Tenochtitlan—the capital of the Aztec Empire—soaked in blood and chameleon cadavers, that the thief is fully integrated in the commercialist temptation, as if to say that the very motif of religious sacrifice itself cannot escape the dialectic of desire, where literally anything can be conquered by the logic of commodity fetishism. Taking up a cross in the marketplace, the thief carries it amidst corpulent Roman centurions gorging themselves on ham to a factory where he allows himself to be cast in plaster, only to awaken later in a warehouse filled with countless life-sized images of himself as Christ. There he throws a fit, thrashes the sleeping centurions like so many moneylenders on the temple steps, and eventually leaves carrying one last statue of himself, which he places on the altar in an old church above a worm- and slug-infested bible. To punctuate the images of a church eaten away by corruption, Jodorowsky then has the thief pull the covers off a bed to find an ancient bishop lasciviously fondling another graven image of Christ. Thrown out of the church by the enraged bishop, the thief then devours the face off his own image before sending it aloft borne by hundreds of blue and red balloons.

As we will analyze in greater detail in the third section, this sendoff of an image of oneself or of a father figure in a recurrent image in Jodorowsky's films and psychomagical practice, and indeed echoes an early action of his own as described in his autobiography. Key here is that the thief's performance as Christ runs up against a sort of internal blockage. The religious sacrifice, the Christological redemption of the violence inherent in the scapegoat mechanism, also fails in *The Holy Mountain*, just as it did in *El Topo*. Both protagonists are still stuck in the dialectic of desire, be it El Topo's inability to eradicate his own violent impulses or the thief's inability to escape the consumerist commercialization of religion and the corruption of the Catholic Church. In all cases, some kind of redemption is desired, some relief from the incessant drive toward unity and lost fulfillment, but that very urge brings nothing with it but eviscerating violence, even when the subject tries to assume it in the form of sacrifice.

The turning point in *Holy Mountain* comes far earlier than in *El Topo*, as the thief, escaping from the marketplace exploitations climbs a tower and encounters Jodorowsky in the person of the Alchemist. After an analytic experience that we will describe in greater detail later, we are introduced to a series of allegorical figures representing captains of industry and government, worldly power—but also with a tint of the seven deadly sins to them, each representing a different planet and excessive ego attributes, such as vanity, political power, sexual desire, aggression, control, etc. All, being industrialists, also express acquisitiveness, or greed. The exposition granted to each industrialist gives Jodorowsky carte blanche for his surrealist impulses, which he explores with relish. A female weapons manufacturer sleeps in a sensory deprivation tank with two women lovers and starts each day by awakening her giant sty full of naked male secretaries. An art dealer and his lover fondle painted sculptures made of human parts, which writhe in ecstasy under their caresses, before using a giant shining pole to stimulate an even larger robotic vagina into orgasm. A fascistic police chief initiates a young follower into his militaristic cult with a ritual in which he cuts off his testicles with shears, before adding them in a bottle of liquid to his shrine. His followers then become the army who descends on student protesters, massacring them as their bodies spew multicolored blood and guts.

This last industrialist is of special importance given our discussion of castration. Yet again Jodorowsky seems to be exploring an analytic concept with a surrealist glee for literalizing the images contained in our words.[35] In this case, however, it is not the primal father who is subjected to the castration by an uprising of his sons; rather, we see the implicit castration of the sons by the father played out as an explicit (in all senses of the word) initiation ritual. A young man is bound, spread eagle on a circular altar in a sun-soaked arena, naked except for a leather sheath covering his penis but leaving his testicles exposed. The camera pulls back to reveal that he is surrounded by military-clad troops playing on drums and rhythmically raising their arms and chanting. Their chief approaches on horseback dressed in a fetish-chic black leather costume leaving most of his body exposed. As his men circle and chant he brandishes a ridiculously enormous toy rifle and mounts the stairs to the altar. In the next scene the gun

THE VIOLENCE OF DESIRE 57

is gone, and he is holding aloft a large pair of shears as he circles the young recruit. We see him hold the recruit's testicles in his hand as he closes the blades on them; but instead of the blades cutting, the film cuts to the recruit's upper body and face as he screams in agony; and then cuts again to the recruit and chief standing together in triumph as they are rushed by the jubilant followers celebrating a new member of their order.

The next scene finds the chief inside a temple, in front of a monumental bust of himself, his arms still aloft in triumph as the recruit comes to him, dressed in a modest leather skirt, holding a bottle in his hands. The chief treats him with tenderness, and the two mount the stairs together as the chief intones in VO that the recruit has undergone the initiation that 999 previous "heroes" had gone through, and that his sacrifice completes the chief's sanctuary of 2 (or "1000 pairs of") testicles, while we see the recruit place a glass with his own testicles floating in clear liquid into the last open space in an enormous shrine of identical containers. He then presents the recruit, as they kneel facing one another, with a small black book inscribed with the chief's symbol, also worn by his other followers, an inverted trident or psi, Ψ, with a circle on top, and tells him it is the holy book.

The inverted trident is itself of great interest and offers multiple paths of interpretation. Of the seven industrialists and their corresponding planets the police chief is associated with Neptune (there is also a weapons' manufacturer who is given the sign of Mars). The sign the police chief has his followers wear has some similarity to the sign of the sea god Proteus, son of Poseidon, who was a shape-shifter able to prophesize the future but unwilling to tell his truth unless trapped and kept from changing forms. In *The Odyssey*, Menelaus informs

58 ALEJANDRO JODOROWSKY: FILMMAKER AND PHILOSOPHER

Telemachus, son of Odysseus, of how he held on to Proteus through several phase changes until he learned from him which god he had offended and of the murder of his brother Agamemnon upon his return from the war. And if the word protean today stems from that god's shape-changing abilities, it perhaps shouldn't surprise us that the same sign was used by Jung to symbolize the unconscious per se, specifically the way our dreams change the shape of our waking reality and express themselves in hidden ways.

Each of the industrialists is associated with a planet and hence an alchemical symbol, but the police chief's specific association with Neptune, the trident, and Proteus suggests that Jodorowsky is here interested in the relationship between our unconscious impulses and the willingness of subjects to be appropriated by state violence, to serve as the willing executioners of a corporate ideology. Indeed, having bound his new recruit via the initiation of castration, the police chief then guides his army into a conflict with other young people, protesting students, where his recruits theatrically slaughter them, covering them with buckets of blood, explosions popping from their shirts, executing them in firing squads, and pulling all sorts of colorful representations of guts from their punctured bellies.

While the commentary on militaristic violence against protesters in a country like Mexico, which had just suffered the trauma of the massacre of hundreds of students by the military in Tlatelolco a few years before, couldn't be clearer, it is also the case that Jodorowsky seems to be delving more deeply into the psychology of violence in this scene. He appears to be asking, what could make one group of young people, soldiers, slaughter another group of young people, even their own compatriots? And his answer regards the "sacrifice" of the young recruit. The gift of the young man's testicles, symbol of his own masculinity, to a leader in exchange for belonging to a group or a cult, is a literalization of the symbolic exchange common to all forms of group initiation. Even at their most basic level, one could argue, governments form this way. Thomas Hobbes's famous image of the Leviathan, the massive power of the state involved the sacrifice of each individual's own power to the state so as, ostensibly, to save each from the privations of the state of nature, where life according to Hobbes, is "solitary, poor, nasty, brutish and short."[36]

But as we now know, most cults also function this way. The followers, once recruited, are expected to give something of value. In the case of some secretive cults like the one led by the Albany-based self-help guru Keith Raniere, NXIVM, the women recruited to be his sex slaves would be required by their "sisters" to give collateral, embarrassing materials that could be used to guarantee their silence and loyalty to the cult. In the crucial moment of their initiation, always performed by another woman to whom they would become eternally bound in a pyramid scheme of submission, they were held down naked on a table and tattooed with a cauterizing pen near their genitals with a symbol representing their leader's initials. It's not surprising that this ritual bears such a strong resemblance to the one imagined by Jodorowsky for the police chief's young militaristic recruits, since both examples imply that what psychoanalysis calls the castration complex is not simply a boy's fear of losing his penis, but a more general problem of binding oneself to a specific set of prohibitions or laws as a way of avoiding the more traumatic truth of one's own very real impotence in the face of a turbulent and unpredictable reality. It's like a man who has suffered from repeated relationship mishaps and who tells his friend he is swearing off sex, to which his friend dryly responds that his deciding not to have sex is like telling the owner of a Fiat that he's not allowed to drive over 150 mph—it's prohibiting him from something he is incapable of to begin with. Or, to put it another way, I comfort myself by telling myself, it's not that I can't do it, it's that I am being prevented from doing it. In the case of the cult recruits, both real and surreal, they accept the cut of the knife and the laws and rules that come with it precisely because the real of their own incapacities is so much more terrifying.

In a fundamental way, giving something of value, or a part of oneself, to the master ties the subject to a larger project, makes literal the implicit claim of the cult, or the corporate entity to which the subject has submitted him or herself: you are nothing without me; I complete you. Entering into this relation to a greater whole implies that one's own partial nature is seen as relative to that whole, as missing only in respect to it. This perceived symbiotic relationship provides powerful impetus for obedience, even in the face of actions that would normally violate the subject's own ethical standards. The women and men who became NXIVM followers and later came to their senses and tried to leave were astonished at what they were willing to do when under Raniere's influence. Likewise, the combination of feeling fulfilled and complete as part of the corporate body and the unconscious desire to fill the part of oneself that has been sacrificed to enter that role, creates a powerful incentive to violence. Not only has the leader soldered the subject's will to his own by taking the sacrifice from him or her, but he has also achieved the effect of directing the inherent violence of desire toward whatever object he deems should be excised.

In NXIVM's case the cult would go to extreme lengths to extort and terrorize members it saw as committing apostasy and now threatening the group with exposure. Those former brothers or sisters would change their attitudes on a dime toward other members once told by the leader that those members were to be considered enemies, and seemingly no punishment would go too far. In the case of Jodorowsky's police chief and his recruits, in a move clearly taken from the Mexican government's demonization of Marxist students that led up to the massacre at Tlatelolco, they perform extreme acts of violence on the bodies of protesters. In both cases what is at stake is the replacement of the will of the leader for what we should, in ideal circumstances, be taking responsibility for, namely, our own desire.

In his *Groundwork of the Metaphysics of Morals*, Kant had insisted on the radical interdependence of duty and autonomy. The core of his system was the understanding that to do one's duty, to do the right thing, can never be the same as following the orders of some authority figure, be it a priest or a king. Indeed, the centrality of this point to Kant's thought is why, a century and a half after he wrote that book, the German Jewish philosopher Hannah Arendt lost her cool in a courtroom in Nuremberg. The year was 1963. Arendt was reporting on the trial of Adolf Eichmann on charges of crimes against humanity for a series of articles for *The New Yorker Magazine* when she heard the defendant try to justify his murder of millions of Jews by invoking the Kantian categorical imperative—which states that only those maxims are moral that can be universalized—and the notion that he was doing his "duty" in following the Führer's orders. As Arendt wrote in her coverage, "This was outrageous, on the face of it, and also incomprehensible, since Kant's moral philosophy is so closely bound up with man's faculty of judgment, which rules out blind obedience." She then added that "Kant, to be sure, had never intended to say anything of the sort; on the contrary, to him every man was a legislator the moment he started to act; by using his 'practical reason' man found the principles that could and should be the principles of law."[37] As we will see in subsequent chapters, the question haunting not only the depiction of fascist corporate violence in *Holy Mountain* but in all of Jodorowsky's explorations of the violence of desire is how to liberate our moral autonomy from the tendency we have to lay it down on the altar of some will other than our own.

Jodorowsky's next completed film as auteur would need almost two decades to appear, but with it he would renew his stamp on the cinematic world with his campy, flagrantly surrealist take on a Hitchcockian slasher film. Despite appearing in a different genre, *Santa Sangre* continues many of the themes from Jodorowsky's previous auteur films—spasmodic violence, fragmented and disfigured bodies, and a love of outsiders and freaks. This time, however, the focus is more on an individual psychology, and on the etiology of a murderous psychosis. Basically, Jodorowsky reimagines Norman Bates, the killer in the British master's *Psycho*, as if he had been the son of an alcoholic American circus-owner and knife-thrower and a Mexican religious fanatic. Jodorowsky's version begins with a young man named Fenix who clearly believes he is some kind of raptor, living in a cage in an insane asylum. Soon we enter into an extreme closeup of his eyes and the film flashes back to his childhood in the American circus run by his father in Mexico City, where we remain for the first third or so of the movie.

THE VIOLENCE OF DESIRE

This long visit to Fenix's past allows us to witness a series of formative traumas. First, Fenix sees the destruction of his mother's church, really a cult dedicated to the heretical shrine to their martyr, a girl who had been raped, her arms severed, and left to die in her own blood. The adherents to the cult believe the girl's blood magically fills a pool in their cheap sanctuary, in which they baptize new followers by having them submerge themselves in white robes, which are then dyed by the miraculous "blood." The local bishop, at first sympathetic to the believers' complaints that their shrine not be demolished by a local developer, reacts in repulsion once he has seen their rituals, calling them blasphemers and quickly agreeing to the demolition. Young Fenix watches in horror as his mother is almost crushed by bulldozers, before running to her side and returning with her to the circus, where she also works as a trapeze artist who suspends herself by the hair (a nod to Jodorowsky's own father, Jaime, who also worked in a circus and had an act in which he hung by the hair).

Fenix is also privy to the mutual seduction of his father, a drunk, barrel-chested knife-thrower with an eagle tattooed on his chest, and the tattooed lady, who lasciviously dances for him and allows herself to be tied to his wooded target as he throws knives around her body and eventually between her legs, to her orgasmic delight. Their dalliance leads to the ultimate trauma, which starts when Fenix's mother witnesses them cavorting while she is suspended by her hair during a performance. Once descended, she finds them in one of the trailers and provokes coitus interruptus by acid bath on his genitals, at which point, before the boy's eyes, Fenix's father kills his mother by slicing off her arms, and then reenacts the post-castration suicide of the Colonel in *El Topo*, staggering for a few paces naked, bleeding between the legs, before taking one of his throwing knives in his hand and slitting his throat.

That El Topo's castration of the primal father in the form of the tyrannical Colonel becomes the castration of Fenix's actual father in *Santa Sangre* makes sense in the context of Jodorowsky's own recollections. In his autobiography he recalls his abusive treatment at the hands of his father, the tyrannical former circus worker Jaime, and the fear it inspired in him—fear that was extinguished only by young Alejandro committing a symbolic act of castration. Having run away from his parents' house, he returned one evening on a hot summer night and snuck into the room where his father and mother lay naked on their bed. There he was shocked to see that his father's penis was not large as he imagined it must be, but smaller than his own. He dumps a pile of dirt and worms on the bed between their legs and departs. When he returns the next day they never mention it, and Jodorowsky's fear of his father never returns.[38]

For Lacan castration is never such a literal relation to the penis or testicles as Jodorowsky makes it in his work, and we can certainly be tempted to think that Jodorowsky's versions are in fact intentionally graphic and literal. For Lacan castration isn't so much a specific anatomy-related anxiety as an existential fact. Castration is equivalent to the phallic function; it is the implicit, unconscious acceptation of symbolic prohibition: I cannot enjoy everything without limit because someone more powerful than me has prohibited it and is using that power to enjoy what I cannot. As mentioned above, however, this symbolic castration is a kind of shield. Rather than limit us it actually protects us from the traumatic truth of our own powerlessness. In reality we are weak and incapable. We wouldn't be able to enjoy everything we wished for even if the prohibition didn't block us, and hence the prohibition supplies us with a pleasurable fantasy. It is for this reason that the sign of castration and the sign of the phallus are one and the same; a kind of protective husk around the *objet petit a*, the sign of castration protects us from its existential lack while tempting us with a trace of its possible presence. We enjoy by tarrying with that sign, orbiting around it.

For this reason Jodorowsky's castration scenes must be read not as literal castrations but as symbolic encounters with the veil protecting us from the far greater trauma of our own impossible reunification with our original lost being. They are, like the horror film watched intently and repeatedly by Chiesa's child, a source of fascination and repetition precisely because they stage the opening/closing of a veil under which liberation, maturity, independence, and the fulfillment of all desires is hoped for but not in fact possible. And indeed in both Jodorowsky's scenes and his recollections, this is more or less how it plays out: El Topo enjoys a moment of triumph, and then dives again into his quest to live up to the expectations of his beloved; young Alejandro experiences some liberation from the fear and intimidation of his father, but soon is beset by other challenges that ultimately lead him to depart Chile for good. Ultimately the fantasy of castrating the father and taking his place is self-defeating; it is yet another manifestation of the violent dialectic of desire. And this is because castration is nothing other than our existential fate of finitude cast as a temporary phenomenon, some day to be overcome.

In the case of *Santa Sangre*, of course, the castration scene is not a revenge or surpassing of the father as in the other cases, but a moment of absolute horror witnessed along with the murder of his mother by young Fenix. Indeed, as he staggers in agony and before taking his own life, the first act of Fenix's father is to pin his mother to the knife-throwing target, take two knives in his hands and swing them both up from under her arms, severing both her arms exactly like the martyred girl of her own fantasy. Fenix watches this locked in a trailer, gazing through the movie-screen shaped back window as his mother, cackling insanely, collapses into a pool of her own blood, before witnessing his father's suicide.

So in Fenix's case, rather than a "normal" unconscious step in a young man's development (albeit a step that confirms the overall patriarchal disorder of belief in the existence of the state of exception to which to aspire), this castration/murder/overcoming of the father is actually witnessed alongside the castration/death of the mother (in her case the arms have become obvious stand-in appendages, which will become important as the plot develops). This confrontation with such a traumatic scenario (nothing is more traumatic than being forced to witness the literal enactment of an unconscious fantasy, since the whole point of the fantasy is to protect from it ever becoming reality) leaves Fenix in his quasi-catatonic state, unable to speak, a grown man who imagines he is the eagle his father etched into his chest on the last day of his life, tenderly telling him through the boy's tears, "Now you are a man."[39]

Again the phrase "becoming a man" is the symbolic trigger for a series of killings. In Fenix's case, delayed/detained by his trauma in a state of quasi-childhood, he crosses into full psychosis and starts to hallucinate the presence of his mother, alive but lacking arms. Lacan's famous formula for psychosis works perfectly here. If in normal

THE VIOLENCE OF DESIRE

neurotic development what is repressed in the symbolic (the name or prohibition of the father, the *non/nom du père*, steps into the place of the unconscious fantasy of pluripotency) returns in imaginary form (as bodily symptom, repetition of a specific failure, etc.), in psychosis what takes place is not repression, but something more profound that Lacan calls foreclosure. In foreclosure, the very function of the name of the father per se never appears; instead of replacing radical, fundamental incapacity with temporary prohibition, the subject loses that mediating function altogether and unconsciously believes he or she already inhabits a world free of any lack, any mediating function whatsoever: "what is not symbolized reappears in the real."[40] Fantasy scenarios (be they of pluripotency or of the presence of a menacing other whose commands we must follow) simply enter our living reality.

This is what happens to Fenix. On the day after a kind of sexual awakening when he is taken on a field trip with a group of children with severe Down syndrome and a local pimp takes advantage of them and brings them to party with prostitutes, he is approached by his mother, who calls to him to follow her. From this moment on the film becomes Hitchcock's *Psycho* from Norman Bates's eyes, as it were, as if we were always privy to the one scene in that great film when we hear Norman and his mother arguing, not yet aware that his mother is a desiccated corpse. In *Santa Sangre* we encounter the mother as Fenix sees her, still young and beautiful, perfectly preserved except for her lacking arms. And here the violence of desire really starts. For Fenix, instead of being permitted to develop normal sexual relations, adopts his mother's attitude and sees every potential mate as a villainous seductress who must be eliminated so as to maintain the perfect symbiotic relationship of mother and child.

68   ALEJANDRO JODOROWSKY: FILMMAKER AND PHILOSOPHER

Fenix's arms and hands become his mother's arms and hands. After first slaughtering the tattooed lady, whom he finds in the same neighborhood where the pimp took him and the children to the prostitutes, Fenix embarks on a new career as his mother's arms. We see Fenix's version, where she sings and dances without arms and he hides, dressed in black like a puppeteer, and moves his long, elegant arms as if they were hers. In the film's diegetic reality, as we will only discover later, there is no mother, only Fenix hallucinating his mother. As he sits behind her so that she can practice piano (and snipe at him for minor failures, naturally), his mother informs him that he exists for her, "You are nothing without me"—the classic line of abusers in abusive relationships who convince their victims to return again and again because they have no subjectivity or independence, they must see themselves as full beings only when together with their abuser. Under the sway of this hallucination Fenix battles his own better angels and kills scores of young women to whom he feels the slightest attraction.

The scenario Jodorowsky created for *Santa Sangre*, while resplendently campy, in some ways encapsulates in its most direct form the kind of violence generated by the dialectic of desire. Obviously this is not to say that it's natural for all of us caught in the dialectic to turn into murderous serial killers. Rather, Fenix's violent psychosis represents in a hyperbolic and metaphoric way the very structure of the fantasy that leads us to engage in damaging compulsions in the first place. In Fenix's case the instances and traumas are all extreme, and hence it follows that the symptoms be extreme. Also, as mentioned above, seeing his dead armless mother, and following her commands to slaughter the women who tempt him, is a psychotic, not normative/neurotic formation. Psychosis literalizes symptoms that would otherwise show up in metaphorical transformations of unconscious impulses. Witnessing his own father actually castrated/ killed as the primal father by the mother who is then castrated/ killed in turn, is simply too much for the young psyche to absorb. It cannot be repressed and rather the literalized fact of these castrations (that the other is now quite obviously lacking) is foreclosed for Fenix. His imaginary reality now becomes seared to his fundamental fantasy, with no room for metaphorical replacements, and he hallucinates a whole new world.

That world has the virtue, for us, of spelling out in detail what the fundamental fantasy for someone like Fenix looks like, and how it structures his particularly bloody version of a repetition compulsion. (Psychotics in this sense, it is said, are relatively easy to interpret, but hell to treat.)[41] In Fenix's fantasy his mother is alive and in a symbiotic relationship with him. She is not lacking anything, because he is her completion. If he is nothing without her, that is so in a literal sense, just as one's arms would be withered relics once detached from our bodies. Fenix becomes his mother's arms in a frantic attempt to complete himself, to fulfill the fantasy that he is something, something whole. In his case murdering young women isn't the fantasy itself, but an unfortunate side effect, a kind of collateral damage of the fundamental fantasy that he is capable of being fused to his mother as a rerecovered, unmortified, whole.

In this way, as different as the stories may seem on the surface, *Santa Sangre* repeats a crucial structure we see in all three of Jodorowsky's earlier films. (As we will see later, the two last films have a somewhat different approach since they are more properly autobiographical and

70 ALEJANDRO JODOROWSKY: FILMMAKER AND PHILOSOPHER

hence the work of a mature Jodorowsky applying a psychomagical approach to his own life story.) In *Fando y Lis*, a couple's desire for unity and completion is subjected to repeated frustration and failure resulting in gendered violence against the backdrop of an imagined fantasy of rebirth and renewal. *El Topo* allegorizes the development of male subjectivity, projecting the brutal results of a patriarchal ideology wherein the man competes for the gaze of the woman in a desperate attempt to prove himself worthy of having a phallus that doesn't exist. *Holy Mountain* shows the same journey as a quest for enlightenment that starts later in the journey than *El Topo*, with the apotheosis of sacrifice that is represented by Christianity, only to move beyond that to show the continued search and subsequent possibilities of self-transformation, as we will explore in the next two chapters.

In each case what is on display is the violence engendered by the dialectic of desire. As humans come into consciousness of themselves and the world they do so through language. The word's magical ability to mean something other than it is permits communication, but it also generates objects that can be simultaneously present and absent, and that carry their potential loss always with them. In other words, the very ability we have to hold something in our imagination as opposed to our senses, which is enabled by assigning it a word, also allows it to exist for us when not there and thus be desired. This basic function of language in turn enables our consciousness of time and ultimately of our mortality, eventually becoming the stage for narratives, theories about the world, our identities, and specifically the sexuated nature of the world we find ourselves in. As these theories manifest in particular ways in each and every individual, they become both the template of our pathologies and the unique palette of ourselves. At bottom, though, whether our adaptations are more or less neurotic—or in particularly unfortunate cases, psychotic—we enter into a dialectical relation with the objects of desire that structure our fundamental fantasies. We desire them because of their promise of reunification with a lost wholeness, a return to Eden before the fall, at the same time as we fear the abyss behind them, the truth of our existential partiality.

As we identify with gender roles, they dictate in a rough way certain tendencies for dealing with the internal contradictions produced by desire's dialectic. The patriarchal structure manifested throughout so many cultures presupposes the universal application of patriarchal values, submission to the law of the father, and the strict division of gender roles, all positing a position that is immune to, and outside, such limitation. We submit, we are conditioned, because somewhere, someone does not submit, is not conditioned. Typically male pathologies flow from this organization: perversions in which the subject claims to enjoy his symptom not for himself but for the Other, in the name of God or the Party, while in fact enacting a kind of parody of the father and using an object or ritual as a way to enjoy by disavowing castration; or obsessive compulsions whose sufferers repeat certain behaviors in certain orders incessantly, often at great cost to themselves, in order to placate the Other, like personalized religious rituals intended to cleanse themselves of sin. Indeed, what are organized religions other than socially accepted mass obsessive compulsions, normalized by time and liturgy?

Typically female pathologies, in contrast, tend to spring from a different positioning vis-à-vis the phallic function. They tend to involve the subject's objective orientation as regards another's desire.

In so doing, female subject positions exhibit a certain ground-level skepticism as to the universality of the phallic function, as though being witness to the other's desire implies he is missing something. No exceptional position is assumed, but at the same time the universality of the law comes under doubt. In an interesting way culture is aware of and registers these differences. Look at the current proliferation of superheroes who themselves more and more exhibit antiheroic attitudes, in that their heroic abilities seem to entail ever more alienation from social and political norms. Naturally, the vast majority of these figures are males, but the contrast with the few female superheroes is telling. And while almost all male superheroes of this stripe are characterized by their willingness, even obsessive drive to occupy society's state of exception, excluding themselves from the very law they relentlessly enforce (think, of course, of the paradigm of this trend, Frank Miller's Dark Knight as popularized by Christopher Nolan's trilogy of films) the few female characters if anything embody an overall skepticism to this very idea of the purity of the law and its universal applicability.

Consider Maya Phillip's take on the antihero phenomenon, in which she succinctly notes these differences from an entirely untheorized perspective:

> [T]he antihero is so often an avatar of traditional markers of masculinity. He broods over his past. He muscles his way through his obstacles, almost always with a six-pack and bulging biceps. He's a rapscallion who can fight the law because coded within the archetype is a male privilege that depicts him as an unstoppable force; he is his own judicial system.

The female antihero (as scarce as they still are) resists being a cookie-cutter figure. She is less emotionally opaque than her male counterparts, but she can be devious. She is willing to break the rules because she realizes the rules weren't created for women like her anyway.[42]

Phillip's observation about the few female antiheroes (she cites Harley Quinn and Jessica Jones) reveals something about the nature of sexuation that deeply informs even our contemporary culture, and that is powerfully at play in Jodorowsky's exploration of the violence of desire. There are in general at least two ways of facing the existential conundrum we are placed in by the dialectic of desire. The one that most fully embraces the patriarchal structure is also the most fully invested in ideologies that can blossom into violence toward others and oneself. The unconscious belief that an exceptional Other underlies an otherwise perfectly universal law, and that this Other is the only thing keeping me from the fulfillment of my lost wholeness, results in a host of symptoms both personal and societal, whose basic structure is lashing out at someone or thing or group that appears to embody the temporary and malicious blockage that keep us from full enjoyment or the repetitive circling of whatever the specific sign of our own separation from the object may be. Whether self-directed and resulting in depression and anxiety, or other-directed and resulting in pain inflicted on other individuals or groups, these are the most direct manifestation of the violence that desires engenders, as the subject internalizes the false idea that it is not that I am intrinsically powerless or fatally flawed but rather some external agent is preventing me from getting my full due.

In some ways the most obvious clinical manifestation of this ideological pathology is phobia. Phobics are psychically effective because they place all their chips into one basket, thus permitting themselves to believe that their lack is not structural but merely incidental, and that were it not for the object of the phobia standing between it and them (whether something innocuous like dogs or heights, or something more pernicious like Mexicans in the United States) they would have access to this pure plenitude. In that sense, xenophobia or homophobia is particularly aptly named both from a clinical and a political-theoretical perspective.

Naturally, the pathologies produced by the female, or other, or non-patriarchal (including non-binary) forms of sexuation also involve suffering. But what is key here, and what we will explore in the next two chapters, is that precisely in the skepticism they demonstrate to the patriarchal order and in their willingness to countenance other ways of being; other possibilities than the law and its singular exception, these subjective structures also show the way to possible liberation from the ego's submission to the dialectic of desire. Not in renunciation of desire, not in its cessation, but in a kind of quasi-analytic or artistic practice that can transform desire into something else, something underlying it and more fundamental, more attuned to the existential fact of our finite and always partial subjectivities. And this is what I will try to show going forward: that in some ways despite himself, despite what appear at times to be reifications of the most patriarchal positions (such as the apparent embrace of a phallocentric understanding of female desire in his portrayal of the character El Topo), Jodorowsky's understanding of art and its power, his practice of psychomagic, evince something entirely different. Namely, they demonstrate in practical, tangible form a kind of philosophy of desire in which certain positions, certain awarenesses, can indeed unravel the dialectic of desire and the violence it generates.

And for all the apparent ratification of gender roles, the irony is that these practices and artistic projection ultimately valorize first a non-male, antipatriarchal approach to human subjectivity and, second, forms of intervention into our psychic and political problems that build on, indeed in some ways directly instantiate, the kinds of interventions theorized by Lacan. Specifically, and as we will explore in detail in the next two chapters, two steps are involved. First, the suffering subject encounters some other subject who steps into the position of a teacher, a guru, in short, someone the suffering subject supposes to know something about his or her problem, his or her deepest self, something even the subject doesn't know. This knowing Other is often cryptic, mysterious, and poetic; but what is essential is that for some reason he or she inspires in the subject a belief that revealing his or her deepest secrets to that subject-supposed-to-know will lead to some resolution of his or her suffering.

This first step is far from uncommon, obviously. In fact most people in history, perhaps all of us, can be described as having succumbed to such a relationship at some point in their lives, if not most or all of their lives in the case of that vast majority of the human race who have subscribed to religious doctrines and given their allegiance to priests and other guiders of the faithful. And indeed it must be added that such seemingly blind allegiance is dangerous. How does one know that one's guru is not a crook, a swindler, a cult-leader, a predator, etc.? In this regard as in others the next step is essential. For the analytic intervention to function, once the relationship of subject to knowing guru has been established and what Lacan called transference has taken place, something needs to occur that radically undermines or disturbs that relationship precisely in the moment when the subject's fantasy of fulfillment is most evidently staged and at its most vulnerable. Something must reveal for the subject the emptiness of that fantasy and thus shift him or her abruptly to a new level of consciousness, a confrontation with the fundamental, constitutive partiality of his or her own existence. This process can be more than unsettling; it can be painful, and it almost always entails the destruction or dismantling of the subject's sense of self, accomplishments, and the basic ruts of his or her life. But in cases where the subject has been suffering self-damage, or in cases where we are damaging ourselves and our planet, such subjective destitution is arguably the necessary step toward what Kant called enlightenment, the emancipation from our own self-tutelage.

3

Staging the Fantasy

In Michael Pollan's book and documentary series *How to Change Your Mind*, the journalist explores the history of psychedelic substances and their potential to change how we go about treating a number of common mental illnesses. One of the experts he interviews is a neuropsychopharmacologist named Robin Carhart-Harris, who points out that the word psychedelic means "mind or soul revealing," a term he finds particularly apt in the context of the effects he studies of psilocybin on human subjects. Psychedelic substances like magic mushrooms, he says, "do truly broaden the lens." While it may be commonplace to think of LSD trips as "expansions of consciousness," Carhart-Harris chooses his words quite literally.

As he goes on to explain, the brain imaging experiments he designed show that "psychedelics appear to be working on the Default Mode Network," the network of areas in the brain that work together to house our sense of self.[1] The potential of psychedelic therapy derives from the substances' ability to break down or disrupt that network. While this would seem to be counter-intuitive—after all, isn't a disruption of our sense of self a good description of a mental illness in the first place?—it turns out that the very network that houses our sense of self can in some ways be understood to be responsible for our mental illnesses. As he puts it, "a lot of mental illnesses appear to be a kind of defensive reaction to uncertainty." By way of an example he cites eating disorders like anorexia, which can be seen as a way of gaining a certain modicum of control for the subject, even if the cost ends up being so great that it could be potentially life-threatening.

Ironically, for all the touted distance between modern brain science and psychoanalysis, Lacan had a remarkably similar understanding of the psyche and the relation between our sense of self, or ego, and mental illness. He was relentlessly critical of the mid-century movement in American psychoanalysis known as ego psychology, which derived initially from the work of Sigmund Freud's daughter Anna Freud, and after her from contributions by Heinz Hartmann. Hartmann in particular had believed that a normally adaptive ego would be largely free of libidinal impulses, and that it was the job of the analysis to help the patient shore up the ego when it was beset by conflict from the id. Lacan, for his part, insisted that such an understanding of the call and purpose of psychoanalysis was a perversion of Sigmund Freud's original vision. Buttressing the ego could not be the aim of psychoanalysis because the ego was, to Lacan's way of thinking, merely the most fundamental of defense mechanisms and, as a result, would calcify into the subject's psychic structure the kind of reaction formations most likely to cause, not hinder, suffering. The ego wasn't the solution, in other words; it was the problem.[2]

The challenge for psychoanalysts was how to break through the subject's defense mechanisms since the ego would sense the analyst's intrusions and go to great lengths to protect its formations. In fact, many of Lacan's clinical innovations were intended as ways to work around the ego's defenses. Take for instance the much-criticized variable time innovation, whereby the analyst makes the length of the analytic session, normally a strict 50 minutes, depend on the circumstances of the analysis itself. The practice was cynically regarded by some as a quick way for Lacanians to cheat their patients out of a few extra bucks, since they could in theory schedule more sessions into a day by shortening them. Naturally, they would continue to charge the same (outrageous) rate, even for the curtailed session. Despite such potential for abuse, Lacan insisted on the benefits of his innovation (in fact, to the point of being kicked out of the International Psychoanalytic Association!), and the reason for his insistence goes to the heart of the rapprochement between his ideas and modern neuroscience.

To explain how variable time sessions work, let's imagine a patient who regularly comes to his sessions and seems to speak uninhibitedly about his life and problems, free associating, and recounting dreams, exactly as expected. As good as he is at his part of the analytic relation, though, the man never seems to make any progress. His basic stories and complaints remain the same; his symptoms never progress. So one day as the 50-minute mark approaches and the man is winding down his narrative, the analyst decides to let him continue, and does not stop the session as he usually would. A minute after the usual ending point the man continues but shows some signs of confusion. Two minutes later he completely breaks down, loses his composure, and for the first time starts revealing aspects of his story that have been hidden even to himself. It turns out that the man had incorporated the length of his sessions into the very fabric of his ego; the time limit had become part of his defense mechanism.

For both Lacan and Jodorowsky, the ego is, as Carhart-Harris might put it, a veritable bastion of defense reactions against uncertainty. One of the major goals in both Jodorowsky's art and practice, as in Lacanian theory, is to expose the basic underpinnings of the ego's investments in a way that is vulnerable to interventions that can alter its structure so as to achieve some kind of therapeutic effect. And in both instances, remarkably similar approaches end up emerging. Specifically, Jodorowsky's art and practice and Lacan's analytic theory and practice converge in the belief that what Carhart-Harris called the Default Mode Network's series of stories and memories that support the self also contains powerful illusions, and that these illusions will resist our attempts to dispel them unless we find a way to break through them and reveal the underlying contradiction and conflicts, the gaping uncertainty lying at the heart of our desires.

The ways both methods find to break through and reveal that fundamental fantasy, thus leaving it vulnerable to intervention, also share profound similarities. In psychoanalysis this involves a necessary first step: transference. Early in its development transference was usually referred to only for its potential negative impacts on the analytic experience. The idea was that during the analysis the patient might start to associate the analyst with people or feelings from his or her past. As a result they might begin to treat them with undue fondness or react in disproportionate anger to something the analyst says. The analysand might even start to develop erotic attractions toward the analyst and initiate attempts at seduction. Even worse, the analyst could end up failing to see transference when it was happening and respond with something called countertransference, in other words, also end up projecting his or her own feelings into the relationship.

When countertransference involved erotic or romantic feelings, this could lead to the classic "sleeping with your analyst" trope, obviously not only utterly destroying the therapeutic process and further messing up the patient, but also a catastrophic ethical violation. In some senses the countertransference at the heart of Brian De Palma's classic thriller *Dressed to Kill*, for all its hyperbolic campiness, hits the mark. For when the analyst allows countertransference to guide his or her actions in the analytic situation, the result is about as beneficial as Michael Cain's character in that film pulling on women's clothing and slicing his patients into pieces whenever he feels the slightest erotic attraction for them.

But while such "countertransference" is always something to watch out for (Lacan rejected the term, insisting there was only transference, which can always work both ways), the reality of transference is much more subtle.[3] The early attitude toward transference was similar to that toward countertransference. Namely, it was something to watch out for and try to counteract or evade if possible, since it was only likely to cloud or disrupt the analytic process. If a patient started to treat the analyst as if he or she were one of the patient's parents, that analyst's supervisor would point out that this was transference and suggest ways to mitigate it. As the practice of analysis evolved in the first half of the twentieth century, this began to change, and analysts started to see that the transference in essence opened a door into the patient's psyche that in a more detached situation might remain closed.

Lacan was one of the analysts who early on realized that not only was transference not a trap to avoid, but it was also in fact one of the main tools the analyst had to effect change in the psyche of the patient. As part of his famed "return to Freud" the French analyst taught annual seminars dedicated to interpreting the Viennese founder's writings, and indeed the first two seminars he taught, from 1953 to 1955, were dedicated to reinterpreting Freud's technique in the analytic setting and to reframing the idea of the ego. In those seminars Lacan made it abundantly clear that the ego was not something to shore up against the ravages of the id, but rather a massive defense system that in many cases could harbor illusions and modes of behavior that were inimical to the subject's flourishing. Transference, for its part, was a tool that would enable the analyst to get a vantage on the ego's foundations and potential vulnerabilities that might remain hidden without it.

But what was the transference, and where did it get its power to create potential change? Transference, Lacan explained, was a bit like a theater, scene, or even stage setting that the patient would put on for the analyst. The stage would indeed be meticulously set, the characters on this stage are figures from the patient's past and its set design dredged from his or her memory. Naturally many of these memories would be constructions and the characters would be written by the playwright, the patient, with the sole purpose of expressing the patient's story, just like the so-called well-made play of the later nineteenth century. And like for the avant-garde of the early twentieth century in whose milieu Lacan came of age, the well-made play the analysand produces before the analyst's eye is a construct, an illusion intended to resist our endeavors to pierce it. Like the avant-garde interventions into art in the early twentieth century, the analyst's purpose must be to undermine the resistances of that well-made play, show how its truth lies elsewhere than where the analysand intends us to look.

STAGING THE FANTASY

But before the analyst can intervene to dislodge the patient's carefully constructed reality, he or she must be able to see the mechanisms by which the stage is set, must see the carefully hidden object of desire with its diametrical contradictions, must see, in a word, the patient's fundamental fantasy. This is where the magic of transference takes place. For with transference the patient's unconscious comes to relate to the subjectivity of the analyst in a very specific way: namely, the patient places the analyst in the position of one who has access to some ultimate knowledge hidden from the subject, the knowledge of the subject's provenance, the subject's ultimate identity, and the mystery of the subject's desire. As Lacan would spell out in perhaps his most famous and influential seminar, the key to enabling the emergence of transference is the assumption by the analyst of the position of a "subject-supposed-to-know."[4]

Once the analyst is in the position of the subject-supposed-to-know, the patient begins to perform his or her play for her, in the unconscious hope of cajoling the analyst into revealing the truth of the patient's desire. In these encounters the subject recounts his or her memories, dreams, concerns, and emotional investments, all in the service of a coherent picture of a self that, for all its suffering and problems, is ultimately justified in experiencing those symptoms; in other words, the patient's self-destructive behavior or repetition of certain patterns or depression, whatever the particular set of symptoms, must be due to a given moment in his or her past, when a mistake was made, or some traumatic event took place, or someone inflicted a harm that is now taking its due.

The parade of memories, images, and theories that emerge from the patient's careful setting of the stage aren't necessarily true or false.

84 ALEJANDRO JODOROWSKY: FILMMAKER AND PHILOSOPHER

They could well be memories that others would confirm, or perhaps reconstructions of something that happened in a completely different way. This is one of the reasons why psychoanalysts tend not to encourage patients to pursue legal action on the basis of memories, for example of childhood abuse, that emerge during analysis, and indeed one of the reasons Freud himself abandoned his seduction theory already in the late 1890s. Such memories may very well indicate an actual crime that needs to be prosecuted, but their emergence in the psychoanalytic setting is not so much about their factual, legal character as about their relation to the patient's fundamental fantasy, the primal set of images that situate for the subject his or relation to the contradictory bundle that is his or her *objet petit a*.[5]

Let's take an example stitched together from a number of case studies. A man is in analysis because he finds himself repeatedly alienating himself from his children, driving them away the very moment when he most wants them to be nearer to him. His analyst explores his past and he reveals that he had grown up believing he was the biological child of his parents only to find late in his adolescence that he was the child of an affair between his mother and another man, knowledge of which was passed on to him unconsciously as a child. This happens through a process in which, as the psychoanalyst Willy Apollon describes it, a child absorbs a hodgepodge of stories, hints, and subtle references that he or she barely notices, but which accumulate over time into a background narration he or she has of his or her origins and place in a family.[6] As a result of this process the man developed a fantasy world focused obsessively on tight, nuclear families in which everyone knows their origin, in which the children looked like their parents and knew exactly where they came from. When he was older, he married a woman and had two children with her, exactly as he had dreamed of doing. As the children grew, however, they exhibited character traits that alienated him, because they seemed to come not from him but from his wife. While he admired those traits that were different, that manifested talents or tendencies he didn't have but his wife did, he also deeply feared and resented these traits, because they unconsciously reminded him of the uncertainty of his own parentage.

In his analysis he started to focus on his analyst as someone who represented the knowledge of his identity he didn't have as a child. The analyst began to embody for him the viewpoint from which he was the fusion of his parents, with no external input, no secrets, and no lack of knowledge. He then strove—even as he revealed for the analyst the stories of his trauma, the moment he found out about the lies she had grown up with—to paint himself as an ideal father whose children retraumatized him again and again by withdrawing from him to take up ways of being that were strange and alien to him. In his stories, however, the analyst was slowly able to make out the contour of a specific and impossible object of desire, namely, a baby who would be the direct embodiment of the man, a virtual clone with no trace of otherness. *Another* person, of his own creation, who would also be the *same* person. In moments when his real children expressed similarities to his own way of being, in moments when he could see himself in them, the man felt resplendent joy, and showered them with affection. When, however, his children would express any individuality, when they would manifest aspects of their upbringing that seemed foreign to him, he would lash out

86   ALEJANDRO JODOROWSKY: FILMMAKER AND PHILOSOPHER

at them violently, causing them to mistrust him and increasing his own loneliness and distress.

In the figure of the baby, idolized at first, but who in time becomes an individuated child drawing the man's anger and rejection, the analyst eventually recognized the man's particular object of desire, the contradictory bundle at the core of his impossible fundamental fantasy. The impossible desire was something along the lines of pure, autochthonous self-generation, a becoming of something new that is at the same time something identical to oneself, generation without degeneration, novelty without time. Because of the very impossibility of this desire, the man had structured a self-story, the ego held together in the Default Mode Network, if you will, whereby his self-fulfillment was always stymied by the resistance of his children to his influence and education. They became the prohibition, the artificial barrier separating and at the same time showing the way toward the fulfillment he had lost but always dreamed of regaining. He would court them in the hopes of glimpsing that fulfillment and lash out at them at every disappointment he received from them. In this way the very ego formation that protected him from the uncertainty, the contingency, the mystery of his own identity, was ultimately the cause of his suffering and the suffering of his children.

By occupying the place of the subject-supposed-to-know, the analyst was able to kindle in the man a belief that his interlocutor held the secret to how he could convince his children to stop pretending they were something else and become the extensions of himself they always should have been, but in so doing, what really happened was that the man revealed to the analyst the contours of his *objet petit a*, he showed how the kernel organizing his fundamental fantasy was simultaneously the promise of utter fulfillment and self-identity, and the resistance to that fulfillment made the very fantasy possible in the first place.

The purpose of this exposition of the psychoanalytic theory of transference is to preface how a very similar dynamic is at work in the films and practice of Jodorowsky, even if the necessary dissolution of the transference may not be as evident in his clinical work as it is in his films, as we will see in the last chapter. To that end let's begin with a few examples of what appears to be transference as they appear in his therapeutic practice. If Lacan's simple statement—as soon as there is a subject-supposed-to-know, there is transference—holds true, then the relationships Jodorowsky establishes with his clients almost by definition become transference. Obviously the same could be said of any kind of guru-follower relationship, and perhaps to some extent to any relationship between a learner and a teacher, assuming the latter is indeed endowed with this position by the learner. The question becomes then what precisely distinguishes these positions?

The first thing to say is that the difference lies in the kind of knowledge the guru or the analyst seems to have access to. Unlike a teacher, but perhaps more like a priest, the analyst and guru claim to know something not merely about a discipline or a doctrine. Rather, their supposed knowledge reaches into the very heart of the subject. They appear to know something about the subject's most intimate self, his or her sins, his or her desires, and the reason behind his or her suffering. The analyst, however, is ultimately distinguished from the priest as well as from any guru or cult leader by a very specific trait.

Lacan was also under some pressure to tell his followers why he wasn't simply another priest or guru, or how his teachings differed from a university professor or even dictator, each of which could be described as being assumed to know something their followers don't. During the May 1968 uprisings in the streets of Paris and around the world, Lacan's seminar had been subject to intrusion by students who were protesting the elite, distanced posture of French academics and intellectuals. As Lucian Goldman would later say to Lacan, "you saw, in '68, you and your structures. It was the people who were in the streets!"—a clear condemnation of the leading intellectual model in France at the time and specifically of Lacan himself, whose return to Freud had been influenced by structuralist linguistics.[7] Soon after those protests a young psychoanalyst would join forces with a radical philosopher and write a blockbuster of a book essentially laying a similar charge against the institution of psychoanalysis in France. Félix Guattari and Gilles Deleuze's *Anti-Oedipus* captured the mood of 1968 Paris in aligning psychoanalysis with other disciplines that perpetuated stagnated power structures and hierarchical models of knowledge. Psychoanalysis held particular responsibility in the way it normalized bourgeois values in its image of the Oedipal triangle, mommy-daddy-me. Its practitioners were labeled by Deleuze and Guattari as "priests" for their fetishization of the idea that the Oedipus complex installed a lack at the heart of being, thereby making explicitly the comparison of analytic communities as similar in some ways to priesthoods, with analysts representing the gatekeepers to some kind of invisible world.[8]

It should immediately be said that both authors also felt a great deal of respect for Lacan himself, and their broadside was aimed mainly at an establishment that Lacan had also criticized repeatedly. Lacan had long established his anti-establishment credentials, having been kicked out of numerous psychoanalytic and educational institutions, often having to change his teaching venue because of yet another expulsion or, as he liked to call it, excommunication. In fact, Lacan eventually decided that anti-establishmentarianism should be inscribed into the very DNA of his methodology, and he suggested that groups dedicated to studying his methods (which would be called, rather sinisterly, cartels) should always include an outsider, and should meet for a limited time before disbanding.

Nevertheless, the protest movement, and the fact that students included him in their image of the establishment, clearly jarred Lacan. When students broke into his seminar and disrupted his teaching, he had responded rather tartly with a now famous line: "Ce à quoi vous aspirez comme révolutionnaires, c'est à un maître. Vous l'aurez" (What you aspire to as revolutionaries is a master. You will have one).[9] Hence it is of little surprise that in his seminar the following year Lacan took on directly the question of the relation of the psychoanalyst to such other teachers, gurus, and leaders, and specifically the nature of their discourses and how those discourses affected the psyches of their followers.

In his seminar Lacan outlined four types of discourse, and called them respectively the discourse of the master, the discourse of the university, the discourse of the hysteric, and the discourse of the analyst.[10] Typical for Lacan, each discourse would be described by a formula. Each formula situated a series of well-known, for Lacanians, symbols—namely, S_1, S_2, S, and a—in relation to each other and to the bar separating conscious from unconscious knowledge. The first symbol, S_1, Lacan called the signifier of the master. In his semiotic theory those master metaphors serve as stopping points for the flow of signification along the signifying chain; but also the signifiers that ground an entire system of belief without themselves having a grounded meaning. S_2, in contrast, represented knowledge itself, the flow of signifiers with which we formulate predicates about the world and debate their veracity. The third sign, a barred S, refers to the subject, dissected by meaning and searching for an answer to fulfill its search and ground its identity. The last symbol, the *objet petit a*, of course, gestures toward that elusive answer, without ever revealing it.

The trick to the four discourses is how the symbols rotate through a series of positions vis-à-vis one another, and either over or below a bar representing the separation between consciousness and unconsciousness. The first discourse, that of the master, positions S_1 in the upper left of the formula, in the place of the speaker; S_2, knowledge, is in the position of the other, or recipient of the agent's discourse; under the bar on the right side, in the position of product of the discourse, is a, the elusive excess of enjoyment; and finally under the bar on the left, in the position of the truth of the discourse is the barred S, the lacking and unfulfilled subject. Here is what it looks like all put together:

$$\frac{S_1}{\not{S}} \to \frac{S_2}{a}$$

In this way the discourse of the master can be read as follows. Someone, in the position of master, issues forth a discourse that HE portrays as uniquely conveying the truth and ultimately grounded in an immobile, transcendental reality. The others, the recipients of the discourse, base their knowledge on this presented truth. They feel their lacking being (the unconscious *objet a* guiding their actions and attaching them to discourse of the master) is to be found by following the master's doctrine. The truth of the discourse in turn is what is masked or disavowed by the master's self-certainty, namely, that they are lacking at heart, non-self-identical, that their discourse is grounded on pure contingency.

Clearly the discourse of the master is nothing other than the very essence of ideology itself. A source of power emits a message conveying an ultimate truth; the receivers are libidinally attached to that message by the belief that it holds some ultimate kernel or reservoir of their own identity; in fact the message covers over its own incapacity, its drastically faulty core. A classic example of this discourse is available in pretty much every political rally, but perhaps most overtly in nationalist rallies such as those held by Donald Trump, where he describes an America whose ills are caused by external invasions (immigrants) and internal weaknesses (liberals and RINOs, Republicans in name only), and whose ills can be cured by him alone. In the S_2 position are his followers who chant "USA!," or "Build the wall!" and feel that their identity as "real Americans" can be safeguarded or returned by their adherence to his leadership and his promise of ridding the nation of those blockages internal and external that are keeping it from being great again. This positioning of his followers in this case situates them as phobics for whom the image of the racial, ethnic, or sexual other becomes something to fear, and something whose exclusion or destruction promises relief from their suffering.

From the discourse of the master there are two adjacent discourses, each indicated by a partial rotation of the formula. The first is obtained by rotating the variables counterclockwise by one position, resulting in this configuration, the discourse of the university:

$$\frac{S_2}{S_1} \xrightarrow{} \frac{a}{S}$$

The discourse of the university purports to be an antidote to the superstitions, fundamentalism, and authoritarian discourse of the master, and for that reason is the discourse that Lacan most associated with the modern era, the era in which capitalism emerges as the dominant mode of production and objective, rational processes purport to replace the authority of masters such as priests or kings.[11] In place of diktat the university offers the dispassionate pursuit of truth. In the formula this is represented by S_2, objective knowledge, being placed in the agent's position, where it can address directly as its receiver the object of all intellectual inquiry, the *objet a* of knowledge that is objective, unadulterated truth. Nevertheless, what underlies the discourse of the university is that its authority also rests ultimately on the intervention of a master signifer, the contingent posturing of authority, claims to status, and expertise that are ego-based and ego-gratifying and ultimately self-perpetuating. If the university's value is established on the repression of such venal qualities (which are of course easy to see in the parade of vanity and privilege to be found on elite college campuses), what is produced by the discourse is precisely wanting, lacking, and desiring subjects, subjects whose very strength is ultimately that they are not satisfied by the trappings of knowledge exhibited by the discourse around them.

A turn of the graph in the other direction reveals what Lacan called the discourse of the hysteric.

$$\frac{S}{a} \to \frac{S_1}{S_2}$$

In this configuration the agent no longer evinces any self-certainty but rather foregrounds his or her own lack of knowledge, lack of grounding. In this respect the discourse constitutes definite progress over the ideological, fundamentalist discourse of the master, even more so than the discourse of the university with its product of desiring subjects. The hysterical subject, however, misdirects his or her requests for fulfillment. Like the protesting students in Paris in '68, like protesters in general, while extraordinarily powerful their discourse is ultimately directed at the symbol of power itself, S_1. It is an appeal, a demand, made to the master, which is why Lacan told the students that they were searching for another master, and would find one.

Nonetheless, the appeal itself, the surfacing to consciousness of the fundamental hysterical question—namely, what does the Other (you, the universe) *want* from me—in essence opens the gateway to a kind of transformational dynamic. It opens the door, in other words, to another occupying the position of the subject-supposed-to-know, to the dynamic that Lacan called transference. Obviously, this discursive position is fraught with risks as well. For one, the very nature of being open to another who occupies the position of the subject-supposed-to-know involves the risk of someone, thing, idea, etc., taking over that position with the purpose of leading the subject to do its bidding, to act against the subject's own best interests. It is the counterpart to any ideological model, religious worship, or cult adherence. If a master replies to the appeal and takes the right position up, then we are right back where we started, with the subject or subjects being *subjected* in the original sense of the word, constituting their identities out of submission to the master's mandates.

However, in risk there is opportunity, and it is here that another possibility opens up. If the right person, with the right intention, and the right technique, steps into the position of the subject-supposed-to-know, that person can end up subtly turning the graphs of discourse by one more quarter turn, resulting in the fourth of Lacan's configurations: the discourse of the analyst.

$$\frac{a}{S_2} \rightarrow \frac{S}{S_1}$$

In this discursive arrangement, the agent occupies the elusive object of desire for the split or hysterical subject, hence transference, where the subject projects all sorts of hopeful or resentful relations on the analyst, where the analyst seems to become for the patient the conscious embodiment of his or her unconscious wish fulfillments. Indeed, this is why clinicians often speak of the opening sessions of analysis as the analyst "hystericizing" the analysand, even if that analysand is an obsessional. In this arrangement, however, something entirely different happens from that occurs in the prior discursive structures. The analyst, unlike the master or the university, refuses to produce knowledge, doesn't hold forth or offer endless speeches with rules and procedures to follow. The analyst listens implacably; indeed, in certain traditional configurations of the analytic space,

STAGING THE FANTASY

famously, the analyst occupies a kind of disembodied voice, seated behind the divan where the patient lies, only occasionally letting his or her presence become known through a question, or even a movement, a sound.

That space, Lacan explains in his early seminar on technique as well as in his later seminar on the four fundamental concepts of psychoanalysis, is designed to allow the subject to project the virtual space in which he or she normally presents his or her character, much like the space of a theater, a stage, a *scene*, to use the cognate from Lacan's French.[12] This space or stage, is not only a space where we are seen and where we see ourselves as seen, but is also the space in which and from which we speak: "it is in the locus of the Other that [the subject] begins to constitute that truthful lie by which is initiated that which participates in desire at the level of the unconscious."[13]

The truthful lie is the utterance that the analysand speaks to the analyst, somewhere off behind him or her, an utterance that has the structure of a liar's paradox, *I am lying*. How is it that a subject can, in fact, utter the words *I am lying*, without balking at the paradox that emerges from a too intensely logical analysis? Think of an actor saying those very lines. The same logic that allows us to separate the I of the character from the I of the actor releases us from the apparent absurdity of the phrase. The same logic, according to Lacan, lies at the heart of the Cartesian subject, that form of subjectivity, as he says again and again, that forms the basis of Freud's discovery. The *I* of the statement *I think* seeks in vain to establish, to permanently fix the *I* of its enunciation, the *I* of its being; one of the ways it tries to convince itself that this being has been attained is through the fantasy it plays out in the space of the other.[14]

It is also truthful, this statement, this lie, because in this very act of enunciation the actor reveals the fundamental discrepancies between the *I* of the statement, that is the *I* of the story being told to the audience, and the *I* of the enunciation, the *I* whom the character's *I* is trying to establish as its own, as the certainty of its own truth. This level of truth, the truth that the character wishes to establish, exists at the level of the actions and words that are exchanged on the stage of the Other, scripted actions and scripted words. This script is another word for what psychoanalysis calls fantasy, the mechanism with which a subject structures its reality in such a way as to cover over the incommensurability between the ego-ideal and the ideal ego, between the models it learns to identify with and the imaginary self it tries to construct. This fantasy is what the subject plays out for the benefit of the gaze of the Other, a gaze that holds the promise of the subject's true being, if only the subject could have access to it.

The analytic situation is intended to bring about transference, in preparation for the intervention, or interpretation, of the analyst. Lacan calls the transference the moment of *closure* of the unconscious, which is to say that if the unconscious is manifested in the slips, gaffes (mistakes in staging) that reveal the tensions underlying the subject's presentation of self, the transference stages the subject's constant efforts to keep that incoherence under wraps. The transference is thus a *repetition*, which could also be understood in the French sense of a rehearsal, of that fundamental fantasy that makes the subject's performance believable to itself, that covers up the distance between the speaker and the words spoken, the body and the image it strives to represent. The gaze of the Other becomes the object and origin of the subject's desire when it is posited as that unattainable perspective from which the ultimate truth of my fantasy, of my performance, will be verified, and in that sense it fills in, shuts down, the apertures, the disruptive events of the unconscious.

The transference is only an enactment of the truth of the unconscious insofar as it is an enactment of its opposite, an enactment or repetition of that fantasy connecting what I am for others with what I am for myself, what Sartre refers to as bad faith and Žižek as the function of ideology. From the ego's viewpoint, however, the analysis is the wrong moment to go into this mode, because just as the character/ego gets into the telling of its story for the benefit of the disembodied gaze, that gaze suddenly becomes embodied; the analyst speaks, or coughs, or makes some apparently significant sound that disrupts the flow of the fantasy scenario and makes the analysand (suddenly stripped of her character) aware of the analyst's *presence*.

In his seminar of 1953–4, Lacan describes this experience in the following terms:

> In extracting it from my experience, I told you just now that at the most sensitive and, it seems to me, significant point of the phenomenon (the transference), the subject experiences it as an abrupt perception of something which isn't very easy to define— presence.
>
> It isn't a feeling we have all the time. To be sure, we are influenced by all sorts of presences, and our world only possesses its consistency, its density, its lived stability, because, in some way, we take account of these presences, but we do not realize them as such. You really can sense that it is a feeling which I'd say we are always trying to efface from life. It wouldn't be easy to live if, at

98 ALEJANDRO JODOROWSKY: FILMMAKER AND PHILOSOPHER

every moment, we had the feeling of presence, with all the mystery that that implies. It is a mystery from which we distance ourselves, and to which we are, in a word, inured.[15]

As we will see in this book's third section, in his later teachings and writing, Lacan will connect (if perhaps only implicitly) this element from his own analytic experience with a concept from Freud's teaching, that of *Trieb*, which Strachey's Standard Edition translated as instinct but French analysts translate as *pulsion*, or drive. In this later work, drive is always opposed to desire, always on the side of the body and the real, as opposed to that of meaning, the Law, language, and the Other. The end of analysis is at this time described as a traversal or piercing of the fantasy through to the realm of pure drive.

For now I am interested in the notion of drive or the experience of presence as it is articulated in opposition to the theatrical schema I have described as the normative mode of being with which psychoanalysis tries to contend by endeavoring to reveal its inconsistencies and thus uncover the level of drive. In this sense, drive and presence are related analogically, in that the experience of drive is to the experience of desire as the spatiality I call presence is related to the theatrical staging of our public, ideologically directed lives. In both cases drive and the feeling of presence produced in analytic settings, as well as in some of the ritualistic practices incorporated by Jodorowsky into his healing practice and cinematic work retain a performative power for the realms of desire and theatricality, in that their relative atavism vis-à-vis these later forms of mediation tends to disrupt the experience of normalcy the later forms support. Just as drive is positioned at the disruption of desire in the analytic relation, presence is concealed everywhere in theatrical spatiality, and retains therein some of the mystical, religious, and magical power that was the norm of the world organized according to its mandates. To the same extent, the normal workings of both desire and theatricality depend on their incorporation of drive and presence: with desire we seek the directness of a contact with the world that we believe we have lost with the primary repression of our drives; in theatricality we search endlessly for the little pieces of the real that constitute our only experience of presence.

To return now to Jodorowsky's filmic and healing practice, from early on he was drawn to ritual, puppeteering, theater, and even poetry precisely because of the power all of these practices have to stage our fundamental fantasies in ways that leave them open to almost magical interventions of presence. As we will now see, each of his films engages the possibility of transference in powerful ways. Moreover, his therapeutic work explicitly depends on it.

In some ways, Jodorowsky considers everything he does under the larger concept of poetry. As a young man he had an encounter that planted in his mind the idea of being a poet, and he identified with that calling ever since. As he explains in his autobiography, and depicts in his film *Endless Poetry*, as a child he was beset by a depression so severe it left him listless and obese—indeed he claims to have weighed over 100 kilos at age eleven (something not reflected in the movie version of his life). His mother, sensing his sadness, hopes to distract him with a pastime and brings him a violin that had belonged to her departed brother. She gives it to him and asks him to learn to play it, but the violin comes in a black, rectangular case that looks for all the world like a coffin, and the boy is driven further into despondency as he is jeered at and called "grave digger" by the shoeshine boys he passes on his way to his lessons.

One day, at the end of his rope, young Alejandro throws the coffin case onto the railroad tracks in a fit of rebellion, and watches as the violin is shattered to pieces by an oncoming train. As the local bums gather to pick up the pieces and make a fire out of the splinters of violin and coffin, an old drunk approaches the boy and puts a hand on his shoulder, telling him, "Don't worry, boy, a naked virgin will light your way with a flaming butterfly."[16]

Jodorowsky recounts this event somewhat like the story of Saul being struck down on the road to Damascus—at which point he changes his life and becomes the apostle Paul—as a conversion event, and one whose power came from poetry. As he writes, "This old man, made into a prophet by wine, pulled me out of the abyss with a single sentence. He had shown me that poetry could emerge even at the bottom of the bog where I was buried."[17] Poetry becomes for the young Alejandro the very symbol of freedom, of escape from the tyranny of his parents, his cruel, homophobic father in particular, who thought all poets were "queers" like Federico García Lorca, even when they talked of loving women. But what is it that Alejandro identifies in what he calls poetry? What is it that gives poetry this power?

We get a clue from a practice that was so central to Jodorowsky's life and intellectual development that he begins his autobiography with a reference to it. The practice is Tarot. The reference with which he begins his autobiography is a coincidence: the Tarot of Marseille, which he would go on to expend so much energy and passion recreating, is composed of 22 arcana, and Jodorowsky was born on the 22nd parallel. He follows on and reinforces this coincidence with a report of a second one, having to do with his name. As he recounts, the teacher he had around the time he learned to read was called Mr. Toro, a name Jodorowsky finds curiously similar to Tarot. Mr. Toro taught the young Alejandro to read using a deck of cards, each with letters on them, which he would shuffle and have the children choose from at random, forming words with the letters they chose.

Jodorowsky reports that the first word he formed in this way was *ojo*, which means eye in Spanish. He then writes that the revelation of being able to read a word, to assign a sound and a meaning to a series of letters, was like a thunderclap to him, "as if something suddenly exploded in my brain."[18] Mr. Toro's comment on his first word also stuck in his memory. "I'm not surprised you learned to read so quickly," he told the boy. "You have a golden eye (*ojo d'oro*) in the middle of your name."[19] The anecdotes, both of his first word and the discovery of poetry at a later and more fragile moment of his adolescence, provide an important key to what Jodorowsky ultimately means by poetry, and how the force of poetry as he understands it would eventually be expressed in his films and practice.

To begin with, while Jodorowsky himself evinces a certain openness or at least agnosticism as to the significance of coincidence, we can quickly dispense with any requirement for gullibility here. The number of people born on the 22nd parallel must be at least in the tens of millions; that one of them might become fascinated with Tarot seems more a statistical necessity than an extraordinary coincidence. That *toro* is particularly similar to *Tarot* is something that would only strike someone invested in Tarot as interesting. And, finally, that the Spanish for golden eye appears in Alejandro **Jodoro**wsky's name, while a pretty cool fact, has as little connection to some ultimate truth in the universe than does the fact that Meg, my mother's nickname, appears in the interstice of my full name, Willia*m* *Eg*ginton, or for that matter that my children like to play soccer and get pleasure from *megging* (dribbling the ball between the legs of) their opponents when they play. In other words, no connection at all.

The point, however, is not that such revelations have or fail to have broader significance; what matters is what a subject makes of them. And this is where Jodorowsky's idea of poetry comes into play. As we went over in the first section, the building blocks of language, the phonetic (and in our western languages alphabetically denoted) chunks called words or signifiers, function in certain ways. They are fundamentally different, for example, from a secret code to be deciphered or from the dancing of bees, both examples Lacan uses to differentiate the particular power of signifiers.[20] Indeed, unlike both of those examples, human language both benefits and suffers from a profound flexibility. Words always depend on context; they always have multiple meanings—perhaps even infinite if you count that meaning as the specific cognitive and emotional reactions of a speaker or listener at any given time. And part of that context involves the relation of words to other words. As Saussure famously put it, language is a field of differences without any positive terms.

As words take their position in our developing cognitive and emotional lives, that flexibility and relationality play a powerful role in channeling our needs, desires, and ultimately our sense of self. What young Jodorowsky discovered as he learned to read, or at least what he later recalled feeling, was the strong attractive relation between the dislodged object of desire upon which his nascent sense of self was built and his unconscious organized, and the very institution and movement of signifiers. In other words, he recognized the drive of signifiers to fill in the open questions at the heart of our being. What or who am I? How did I become this way? A teacher, a subject-supposed-to-know, offers an enigmatic and promising solution. Written into the very signs of my name is a phrase, golden eye, that suggests an ability and a destiny. It is something to guide me and to reach for. It is also, crucially, something that retroactively attains significance, a quilting point, a metaphor, and a stand-in for the absence that guides the very movement of desire.

As Jodorowsky grew and further identified himself with poetry, he teased out the kind of uses of language that he found most meaningful. Unsurprisingly, he was attracted to surrealist poetry specifically. He read García Lorca incessantly; a shot from *Endless Poetry* shows him secretly intoning the famous lines from *Romance sonámbulo*,

Verde que te quiero verde.

Verde viento. Verdes ramas.

El barco sobre la mar

y el caballo en la montaña.

[Green how I love you green.

Green wind. Green branches.

The boat on the sea

And the horse on the mountain.]

before his violent father bursts into the room and rips the book from his hands, calling García Lorca *marica*, a slur for a gay person, and telling young Alejandro that he too will turn out queer if he reads such drivel. Not to be dissuaded, the young Jodorowsky continues

104   ALEJANDRO JODOROWSKY: FILMMAKER AND PHILOSOPHER

to write poetry in secret, to memorize his poems, and at least claims to remember some of them today.

Like the first lines of "poetry" he recalls being uttered by the drunk in the street that fateful evening, the poetry he composes is classically surrealist: largely free verse, highly imagistic, and suggestive of potential meaning without being even close to determinant. In other words, these are verses that convey something about the very power of language itself, namely, its extraordinary ability to adapt itself to the interpretive and often unconscious designs of the listener. We see this in how Alejandro embraced the identity of poet after the event with the drunk. That evening he dusted off his recycled typewriter and revolted against his father's sneers by typing out his first poem. "Poetry," he writes, "brought about a radical change in my behavior. I stopped seeing the world through the eyes of my father. I was allowed to attempt to be myself. However, to keep the secret, I burned my poems every day. My soul, naked and virginal, lit my path with a butterfly on fire."[21]

The key to poetry, and specifically the poetic form that called to Alejandro, was its ability to transform reality. In other words, for Jodorowsky, "poetry" refers to the subject's projection of a subject-supposed-to-know onto the contingent play of signifiers, which allows the subject to learn something about himself by what he sees in certain linguistic coincidences. The signifier "poetry" thus refers to an act of transference established not with a single person, but with the entire signifying chain. What Jodorowsky was discovering is that the world we grow conscious of as we enter into language isn't an objective, unadulterated reality, but rather one that has taken on the color and values of the language we have been given to describe it. As he writes later about his first long conversations with the poet Enrique Lihn, who would become one of his first close friends and collaborators, "we both agreed that the language we had been taught carried crazy ideas. Instead of thinking correctly we thought distortedly."[22] He then gives a few examples of the distortions of everyday speech and how they would endeavor to correct them in their own speech. Instead of *never*, they would say *very few times;* instead of *always*, they would say *often*, etc.

Clearly what Jodorowsky and Lihn were encountering was the prevalence of what we could call dead metaphors in our language, the way objects and experiences and feelings that had once been expressed in a new way become, with time and use, the unnoticed wallpaper of common, daily, and lived experience. Their first series of poetic interventions, they decided, would be aimed at disrupting that common language, tearing through that wallpaper, reminding themselves and those around them that the image of reality we have baked into ourselves is conventional, contingent, and ultimately may not reflect our true self or desires. Communication between two people ensconced in our common use of language is like "a conversation between deaf people who do not even know how to listen to themselves."[23] (The ableism in Jodorowsky's choice of metaphor here is indicative of his age, which is an explanation rather than an excuse.)

Thus began a kind of process of internal liberation. "I proposed the poetic act as a solution to this grotesque communication." Unlike written poetry, which Jodorowsky and Lihn thought of as more of an internal, solitary process of liberation and creation, poetic acts were intended to be a "social exorcism in front of numerous spectators."

106 ALEJANDRO JODOROWSKY: FILMMAKER AND PHILOSOPHER

As he goes on to describe in greater detail, in a scene he also recreates in *Endless Poetry*:

> Our intention was to demonstrate the unpredictable quality of reality with these poetic acts. Lihn and I pulled ground meat out of our pockets at a meeting of the Literary Academy, flinging it at the worthy attendees while giving cries of horror. This caused a collective panic. For us, poetry was a convulsion, an earthquake. Appearances were to be denounced, falsehoods unmasked, and conventions challenged.[24]

There is a reference in this quotation, almost certainly intentional. Jodorowsky was a devoted surrealist as a young man. He left Chile for France with the intention of joining the surrealists, by then quite aged but still unchastened in their disdain for convention and conformism. Specifically, he and his friends—for example, the Spanish playwright Fernando Arrabal, the author of *Fando y Lis*—joined André Breton's still-active surrealist group in Paris for several of the last years before the great artist died. And it was Breton who had famously written a new and shocking definition of beauty toward the end of his novel *Nadja*.

As Breton had worked out in his several manifestos in the 1920s but also in the text of his enigmatic novel, surrealist art, or poetry in general, functions primarily as a way of tempting its interlocutor, its reader or viewer, to lay down his or her interpretive guard, to render vulnerable the expectations with which we encounter the world as ready-made, as already meaning something, and thus to permit them to be shattered and replaced by something else, something authentic:

Beauty is like a train that ceaselessly roars out of the Gare de Lyon and which I know will never leave, which has not left. It consists of jolts and shocks, many of which do not have much importance, but which we know are destined to produce one *Shock*, which does … The human heart, beautiful as a seismograph … Beauty will be CONVULSIVE or will not be at all.[25]

Convulsion, a seismographic reading of the earthquakes that poetry can incite in the human heart—Jodorowsky, already a reader of García Lorca, would know those words and make a conscious connection to the surrealist master, and to his idea of beauty, common to himself and his movement but also to others of the European Avant-garde, for instance the futurists, whose leader Filippo Tommaso Marinetti had already in the 1930s become a presence in Latin America's Southern Cone.

In fact, Marinetti comes to mind when Jodorowsky described the event that led him to "discover surrealism" and immediately to describe poetry not as a principally verbal medium but as an act. At one particularly tense dinner table, where such fights between his parents often would break out but usually lead to his father physically abusing his mother, Jodorowsky describes his mother reacting in horror to his father eating, before murmuring, "This man looks like a pig; it makes me want to throw up." Jaime at first merely turns pale, but then raises his plate and throws its contents at her face. When Jodorowsky's mother Sara successfully ducks, the fried eggs on the plate pass over her head and land on the painting behind her, a completely standard Andean landscape that Sara had purchased because her mother suggested it to her. At that point Jodorowsky exclaims, "The two yolks stuck there in the middle of the sky like twin suns. And oh what a

108 ALEJANDRO JODOROWSKY: FILMMAKER AND PHILOSOPHER

revelation; for the first time this vulgar painting appeared beautiful to me! In one fell swoop, I had discovered surrealism. Later on, I had no trouble understanding the words of the futurist Marinetti: 'Poetry is an act.'"[26]

Putting aside the easy conflation of what were in fact two separate avant-garde movements, these anecdotes help us see what Jodorowsky means by surrealism, and what attracted him to its notions of beauty and artistic expression. In each moment from his recollection, Jodorowsky focuses on a random occurrence that leads to a disruption in the flow of conventional life, and that in turn allows for an interpretation on his part, an interpretation that institutes a kind of turn or reassessment of his normal course. As he develops first as an artist and later as a healer, these two steps will coalesce in Jodorowsky's method as distinct moments. The moment of interpellation, of being called by an Other, be it a text, an event, or the words said by a specific person; and the moment of interpretation, where the event, text, or person's intent are read in such a way as to lead to a deviation from a previously set path. The actions he later learns to construct for his patients, many of which he had previously thought of or designed on the basis of his own poetic manipulation of memories, serve as catalysts for the patients to do the same with the ruts of their own stalled lives.

Jodorowsky distills these ideas beautifully in yet another commentary on an event he recalls from his early childhood in Chile, when a man from the local Chinese community that his father has taken to calling the Prince, because of his elegant grooming and garb, agrees to let the Jodorowsky family witness him singing Chinese opera. At first excited about the prospect, his mother devolves into an apoplectic fit when the Prince appears as a Princess, completely flouting gender expectations and singing, Jodorowsky describes, not in "a human voice, but the lament of a millenarian insect." For young Alejandro, the performance is revelatory, "I forgot I was watching a human; before me was a supernatural being out of a fairy tale bringing us the treasure of his existence." His mother seems to have had an opposite reaction, though, "with her face red and her breath coming in short bursts." Jodorowsky realizes she simply could not grasp or "accept the idea of a man playing at transforming himself into a woman."

Indeed, gender nonconformity will play an important part in his later work, even as Jodorowsky himself seems at time to struggle with and in part accept the idea of "eternal" gender forms. The way out of this contradiction, I will suggest, is to see that Jodorowsky is inhabiting simultaneously both sides of Kant's antinomy. On the one hand, part of his analysis of the violence of desire requires acknowledging the power of gender identification, which he does in criticizing his mother's reaction here, and which he also does when, in films like *El Topo*, he stages the violent confrontations of his male character with his own normative gender identifications. On the other hand, Jodorowsky also clearly sees the value of the not-all, the position from which the myths of the phallic function are dismantled. In the end, it may well be that the suffering subject's cure involves reaffirming a gender stereotype, as does the man who Jodorowsky cured of his stutter at least in part by emphasizing his embrace of his manhood, a manhood explicitly conjoined with gender stereotypes such as power and authority. But it also seems clear that, given the specifics of the case in front of him, Jodorowsky would be equally open to having a subject—stage an action intended to discover and then affirm a non-gender conforming identity, as long as that identity were authentic—that is, as long as it were in conformity not with externally imposed social expectations, but with how the subject had organized his or her unconscious desires. Similarly to psychoanalysis, in other words, the ethics of psychomagic would seem to be expressible along the lines of Lacan's famous dictum, "the one thing one can be guilty of is giving ground as to one's desire."[27]

Given the undeniable fact that unconscious desires are also guilty of producing the suffering in question, though, it is essential to distinguish what precisely counts as authentic and what is inauthentically imposed from the outside, as it were. A difficult question to say the least, especially when one considers that in some profound sense all of our desire, indeed all our subjective makeup, is inauthentic in that we become subjects in the field of the Other, under the influence and acting for the gazes and desires of those around us. Here Jodorowsky and Lacan seem again to be on the same page. To be authentic is to acknowledge the very otherness at one's core, to see that the claim of the phallic function to be written in the tissue of the universe and our own claim to be ultimately determined by that code are mere excuses. For authenticity is ultimately self-creating, self-invoking; it doesn't pass the buck to some other who made me that way, the way that everyone must be. It invokes, in other words, a kind of self-birth and willingness to take responsibility for that self-birth.

Indeed, in this respect it is not surprising that in several of Jodorowsky's actions, something like self-birth, or at least a restaging one's own birth under renewed circumstances, takes center stage. One action was designed for a young woman with severe depression, who suffers because she feels that her mother has never loved her and her father is totally closed in on himself and doesn't care for her. Her mother, she goes on, has always blamed her, and told her that she, the child, is incapable of loving her mother. She believes that her mother always treated her as an adult, and that she has been obliged to live as an adult her entire life. Her symptom now manifests as a fear of becoming a mother herself. After asking her the question from off screen, "Do you love yourself?," to which the girl has no answer, the film shows the action he designed for her, titled birth-massage. In it, Jodorowsky's helpers, a middle-aged man and woman dressed entirely in white, first massage and then cut the girl's clothes off with scissors. Then, after tying a brightly colored "umbilical cord" around her waist, they position her in a fetal position between the legs of the now naked female helper and cover them both with a blanket. When the girl emerges from under the blanket and from between the woman's legs, the "parents" now cuddle and hold her like a newborn, giving her every sign of the love she felt she missed as a child. The "mother" then cuts the umbilical cord, and pulls the girl to her breast, where she gives her a glass of milk to drink as if coming directly from her own nipple. They then slowly raise her to her feet and gently "teach her to walk" until she is standing and walking on her own: an entire infancy replayed in a matter of an hour.[28]

In the exit interview that follows the girl appears changed. She begins by recounting that she is now happy, that she feels she loves herself more than she did before. She feels no anger or hatred toward her parents anymore. In this particular case the evidence for a lasting cure is rather strong, given that she then appears, six months later, raising her dress to reveal an authentic pregnancy.

112   ALEJANDRO JODOROWSKY: FILMMAKER AND PHILOSOPHER

While the action of self-birth in this case reenacts for a depressed child the feeling of being wanted and loved by her parents, it is also a kind of literalization of the notion of authenticity that drives all of Jodorowsky's artistic expression from his earliest days coming to consciousness as a poet and artist. Reflecting back on the performance of the Chinese opera singer and his parents' scandalized reaction, Jodorowsky writes this:

> Thinking again and again about this tense situation, which left an indelible impression on my memory, I realized that every extraordinary act breaks down the walls of reason. It upends the scale of values and refers the spectator to his or her own judgment. It acts as a mirror: each person sees it within his own limitations. But those limitations, when they manifest, can cause unexpected bursts of awareness. "The world is as not as I think it is. My ills come from my distorted vision. If I want to heal, it is not only the world that I should try to change, but the opinion I have of it."[29]

Let's think of Jodorowsky's actions, while also clearly based on his patients' narratives, as precisely such "extraordinary acts." Indeed, it is hard not to feel uncomfortable watching a grown young woman being disrobed by two older people, no matter how kindly they seem, and then having her birth recreated, right down to the first sucking from her new mother's breast! In some ways, while utterly "reasonable" in the sense that we can immediately grasp the logic of the reconstruction, such actions also break down the walls of reason and upend the scale of values. Indeed, all of Jodorowsky's actions, like the majority of what occurs in his films, are united precisely by their capacity to shock, even today, when much surrealist art of the early avant-garde has long

STAGING THE FANTASY 113

since lost that capacity. In a recent class for Hopkins undergraduates on the long century of surrealism, my students were unanimous in them feeling that the only truly shocking, truly uncomfortable experience for them, in a course that included Dalí, Buñuel, Ionesco, and many, many more, was watching *The Holy Mountain*. As one of my students, who watched the film early, reported to the others, "I made the mistake of trying to eat dinner while watching it." She also reported difficulties sleeping the night after.

The actions, then, like scenes from his films, are intended to upend scales of values, as he says, with the purpose of creating a mirror in which to see one's own limitations. The action, the scene, in other words, renders visible an implicit framework we have simply accepted without questioning. The shock value isn't incidental; it's a feature, not a bug. In the case of the young woman staging her own rebirth, yes part of the value is to "relive" an infancy she feels she never had. But it would be simplistic in the extreme to believe that a mere reenactment would have the healing power this action evidently did. Rather, what is at stake in this and other actions and scenes is the making visible of previously invisible frameworks of acceptability. Of course, as his parents would tell him, "men should behave like men" and not suddenly appear as the most beautiful princess and sing in otherworldly voices! And precisely because this was such a deeply held belief at the time, the performance shocked Jodorowsky's conservative, traditional parents, especially his mother, but also gave young Jodorowsky insight into the limitations of his upbringing. Today, in our society and an age of ever-increasing (if far too slowly and in too limited a manner) acceptance of queer and transgender people, it takes more than mere cross-dressing to shock; and yet in

114 ALEJANDRO JODOROWSKY: FILMMAKER AND PHILOSOPHER

both his films and his practice, Jodorowsky clearly still manages to do so, and to get some value from this "shock therapy."

In a similar action but this time one staged for a couple, Jodorowsky manages to increase that shock value, all while treating a different kind of suffering. In this case the patients are a middle-aged couple who report that their relationship is in serious crisis. The woman, who recounts having been neglected and abused as a child, appears distraught that she is unable to love her husband. The man, who in contrast lived a happy life as a child before having that happiness ripped away from him by the death of his father when he was nine years old, finds he is missing something in his life, "I feel a lack," he says, "I feel an enormous lack."

In the treatment he designs for them, Jodorowsky again has his "parent actors" stage their births, individually. In the case of the man, there is something truly shocking about seeing a naked grown man emerge "from the vagina" of a woman not much older than him, being helped or even pulled out by another grown man. After some initial loving cuddling with "his parents," he and his "father" play and rough house together, the way he had described to Jodorowsky how he would play with his real father before he died. Again, the camera is merciless, and witnessing a grown man, entirely naked, pretending to be a small child while horsing around with another grown man who is supposed to be his father, is unsettling to say the least. But knowing the man's story and seeing him dissolve into his father's arms in joy, is also quite moving.

In their case the after interview, where yet again like other patients they seem to have revived from the depths of their initial suffering almost completely, is particularly interesting. Both concur that as a result of the action, "it's as if we were confronted even more closely with our problem." The woman then adds that she has come to realize that she needs a change and needs to be recognized and loved as a woman. She adds that at this point the relation could continue or could end, and that in recent days she has been tending to think more that it should end. Jodorowsky then adds a new action to their treatment and has the two walk through the streets of Paris dragging chains from their ankles. The scene is long, and after a few minutes, you realize that, perhaps on their own accord, the couple have started walking off in different directions. They then meet again in a strip of public garden near the Seine, together bury their chains beneath a potted flower, and then embrace and go their separate ways.

What is crucial to recognize in these and other scenes is the role played by the initial interview or interviews, in which the traumas and individual stories are laid out. In these scenes the camera, we the audience, as well as Jodorowsky, who is behind the camera, are essentially playing the role of analyst. We have become, for the patients, the subjects supposed to know, and a kind of transference has developed. In relating their past traumas, the objective truth of what they are recounting is less important than laying bare the structure of the fundamental fantasy. In the woman's case, the neglect by her mother, who expressed to her that had she not been born at home she would not have believed she was her daughter, and the sexual and physical abuse by her father left her with a feeling of having never been a child. The man, in contrast, lost his loving and playful father when he was too young, when he still desired more. He describes himself as still being a child at heart, as unable to accept that he has now become a man.

In a curious way their two fundamental fantasies circle and attract each other like two ravenous black holes, latched at the center by their mutual gravitation pull. The man's lack of adulthood pulls him toward a woman who never was a child; her lack of childhood attracts the man who never grew up. And yet their fantasies and the roles they fulfill for each other in those fantasies end up reinforcing the very blockages that make them suffer. The man continues to feel a lack and cannot self-actualize as an adult; the woman still cannot love, just as she could not love her neglectful mother. Stuck in their pattern, they make themselves and each other suffer. The actions Jodorowsky designs for them, aided by their trust in the subject-supposed-to-know, bring to light the nature of their problem, make them confront it more closely, as the man says. In Jodorowsky's words, the action "upends the scale of values and refers the spectator to his or her own judgment. It acts as a mirror: each person sees it within his own limitations."

As in other scenes in his documentary, Jodorowsky pairs this one with a brief scene from one of his films. In this case it is *Fando y Lis*, a scene in which Fando abandons a wailing and immobile Lis and runs frantically up the hill around her, searching for something he is not finding in her. The parallel between the film's portrayal of a couple in distress and this real couple is not gratuitous. As we discussed in the last chapter, *Fando y Lis* stages the violence of desire, the unconscious eruptions of destructive emotions when the person on whom we choose to deposit our impossible and self-contradictory object of desire fails, as she or he must fail, to fulfill that impossible ambition, the ambition of completing us, restoring us to some initial imaginary completeness. (In repetition, an analyst friend of mine says, the subject stages again and again the same scenario in hopes that the denouement will be different this time, but chooses the protagonists so carefully that the denouement can only be the same.) As Lacan famously put it, "il n'y a pas de rapport sexuel," there is no sexual relation, and precisely as the depiction of a successful sexual relationship is the fundamental ideological gesture of most cinema, the depiction of its failure in *Fando y Lis*, becomes a radical and deeply disruptive gesture.

In order to work one's way out of the dialectic of desire, the first step is a staging of the fantasy that brings into relief our desire in its self-destructive pattern. If in the psychoanalytic relation that staging occurs through the power of transference created by positioning the analyst as the subject-supposed-to-know, the psychomagical relation produces that effect during the very first interviews. Jodorowsky's actions then stage the fantasy, often with almost violent literalizations, in a way that allows or forces the patients to confront their problem more closely, and to see their own limitations. It is as if he understands precisely the care with which subjects choose the protagonists in their own dramas in order to repeat their compulsions, and then stages scenarios that cause the repetitions to fail.

This begs the question of what, in his films, serves the function or plays the role of the subject-supposed-to-know. Is there, in other words, transference at play in Jodorowsky's films? In his earliest film, *Fando y Lis*, there does not appear to be any direct correlate of a person occupying this position, as there clearly are in later films. Nevertheless, like the reader or viewer confronting a book by Breton or a painting by Dalí, one could argue that the surrealist nature of the work itself assumes that function, at least for the spectator. As in any art-consumption situation, we enter that relation searching for meaning, and project onto the work a certain ultimate answer to that quest. If we don't know, at first glance, what the work means, we assume that the work knows, and we engage with it to try to wrest that meaning from its obscurity.

In the case of *Fando y Lis*, the protagonists themselves seem to be in a similar situation. It is as if they themselves, ensconced in their dream-like, at times nightmarish reality, are also at a loss for understanding it, and thrash around seeking for answers. The mystical land of Tar, as outlined in the prologue, takes the place of that object of desire, but unlike in a straightforward political discourse, it doesn't present itself in any obvious way. There is no charismatic leader pointing the way to Tar, only Fando's desperate belief that Tar exists and that the couple must arrive there if their desires are to be fulfilled. Thus if the film and its bizarre diegetic world become the subject-supposed-to-know for us, the audience, and hence engender a kind of transferential relationship, wherein we project our own particular or even pathological fantasy scenario into the lacunae of its semi-coherent narrative, in a parallel way that enigmatic landscape presents the same open question to its protagonists. Fando and Lis become both participants in, and viewers of, a surrealist world that, like the drunkard's poem that ignited young Alejandro's desire to change his life, interpellates them and us by positing within its fold the key to both its meaning and our own.

As Jodorowsky progresses in his filmmaking, however, the function of the subject-supposed-to-know becomes more explicit. The log line for his second film, *El Topo*, could be something like "troubled and violent young gunslinger seeking enlightenment tries out (and kills) four analysts before deciding to set out on his own." Indeed the titular gunslinger, spurred on by the woman whose admiration he craves, confronts four "masters," and in each case enters the duel with them as though he were entering some kind of apprenticeship. Each seems unbeatable before he fights them; each seems to hold some profound secret that, by defeating them, the gunslinger will be able to access. (In some ways this process mimics the tendency often seen in analysis whereby the analysand's resistances manifest at first as an outright rejection of the analyst—he or she is a dud, someone who can't possibly understand the analysand's problems.) In the first instance, the master looks like a fakir, and has so trained his body through meditation that he can open it to let bullets pass through it safely. The second master lives in a caravan with his mother and pet lion. His skills are such that when El Topo tries to draw on him, he easily pulls first and shoots the gun out of El Topo's hand without harming him. He then aims at his heart, but instead of shooting says, "Boom, you're dead. Technically you're dead. But now I want to talk to the dead man."

He tells El Topo to follow him, and then shows him his workshop, where he tells him that at first he learned to work with copper, making his fingers strong. He then shows El Topo a tetragon made of tiny pieces of wood and tells him that he later progressed to making delicate objects, and that his strength now consists in being able to play with such an object without damaging it. While talking he tosses the object around in his hands, and then passes it to El Topo, who breaks it the moment he touches it. He then tells El Topo to shoot at another such shape in the distance. El Topo does so, destroying it entirely. When the master shoots at another one, he is able to remove one tiny piece with his shot, leaving the rest of the structure intact. He then tells him, while violently beating him up, "You shoot to find yourself. I do it to disappear. Perfection is losing oneself. To lose oneself, one has to love."

In this encounter the new master has clearly once again stepped into the position of the subject-supposed-to-know. He demonstrates an ability El Topo wants but cannot yet attain; he speaks enigmatically, as if in parables; he positions an object of desire inside himself, the knowledge of how to, in this case, become the perfect gunslinger. Paradoxically, the knowledge seems self-defeating, for a gunslinger. You have to learn to shoot not to destroy, break, and kill, but to disappear, to lose yourself. As we will see in the next section, having the loss of self as a goal and a requirement for advancement is crucial, and completes in some ways the parallel between Jodorowsky's aim and the method designed by Lacan. For now, however, the second master's words can be seen as establishing the sway of something like transference, in particular in his mention of love.

The master tells El Topo he cannot win because he doesn't lose himself, which requires love. El Topo doesn't love, he continues, "you break things, kill, and no one loves you." But he also has a special strength that makes him dangerous: "you no longer fear dying." In some ways it is clear that what is at stake here is transference, or specifically, the failure to fully achieve something like transference on the part of El Topo. As Lacan says in many places but works out most fulsomely in his seminar on transference, to love is to give what one doesn't have, it's to make a gift of one's very lack and, specifically, to give that gift to someone who doesn't want it.[30] We can see from this formulation that love involves something more than desiring something or someone. Where desire entails the promise of fulfillment in an object that cannot possibly carry that weight, love requires one to represent one's own lack to another and receive back from that person a mirror image of that lack, something one doesn't want to see. The love relation involves two lacking subjects who recognize their own lack in each other, rather than see in each other the ultimate possible restitution of a loss.

When he stands on the precipice of defeating El Topo, the second master instead offers him love. He shows his vulnerability, his own lack. He reveals his love for his mother specifically. "I've given myself to her. I've told her everything. She's inside me," he intones while caressing his mother's foot. "Her infinite love fills me." "I hate all that is mine, because it distances me from her divine presence." But in so revealing his own love, the master has placed a fatal weakness in the sights of a man he has already recognized as dangerous, because he doesn't fear death. And El Topo takes advantage of the opening. Not loving himself, not representing his own lack, in other words, El Topo doesn't reciprocate in any way the second master's trust and opening. And while already defeated by him in skill and strength, he uses his cunning to kill him—precisely by distracting him with the second master's own object of love. When the mother rises to give him his pistol back, telling him that her son has decided to give him a second chance, she steps with her bare foot on some sharp shards El Topo has placed beneath her. When her son rushes to her aid, El Topo takes his weapon and shoots him from behind, leaving his dead body sprawled before the screaming mother.

The theme that El Topo no longer fears dying, and that this makes him a dangerous enemy, is reinforced in the next challenge. The third master lives a peaceful, simple life, dressed in white, taking care of his rabbits. El Topo crosses over the fence around his enclave with his hands raised, leaving his gun behind. The master quickly corrects him, telling him that he trusts him, and that he didn't need to disarm himself. Then he takes out a small violin and tells El Topo to take out his flute, so that they can make music together. Then he begins to analyze him. "You are disgusted at yourself," he tells him. "You don't want to betray any more. Now you want to respect the law." Then he goes on to talk about the gifts that people bring him. "Some give flowers, some precious objects. You bring me your life as a gift." And it is here that he repeats the theme of El Topo's great strength: "You are no longer afraid to die. That is why you are a dangerous enemy."

But of course, what makes El Topo dangerous is precisely not what would allow him to progress to some kind of enlightenment. Not fearing death, or fearing it less than his opponents, puts El Topo in the place of the master in Hegel's dialectic. He wins over his opponents, but in so doing he places himself, or seeks to place himself, in the position of absolute master, to be served by others. This attitude is reinforced by the woman, who is always at his side before or after his duels, telling him not to leave her. But the master, as Hegel reminds us, remains in the dustbin of history. It is the servant who, by fearing death, by subjecting himself to the will of the master and working the land for someone else's use and pleasure, transforms himself. El Topo confronts the masters, but always with a trick, always with a mind not to truly submit himself to their teaching, but to dominate them. He does not, in other words, accept them as subjects-supposed-to-know but assumes he already has the knowledge himself. In the case of the third master, El Topo, knowing in advance that the master's shot will

STAGING THE FANTASY

flawlessly go to his heart, covers his heart with a small copper dish he took from his previous duel. After pretending to die, he then rises and kills the now defenseless master.

For his fourth and last challenge El Topo at first seems to be up against more than even he can handle. An ancient hermit sits alone in the desert and laughs at the suggestion that El Topo wants to fight him. With what, he asks since he long ago exchanged his revolver for a butterfly net. The old man then suggests they have a fist fight and provokes El Topo to try to hit him. Soon the gunslinger realizes he can't touch the old man, who is far too spry and cunning. When he pulls his gun on him, the old man again laughs, and deflects his bullet with his butterfly net, before warning him, "If you shoot again I'll reflect the bullet directly into your heart." At this point El Topo sinks to his knees, and the old man informs him that there was no way to win against him, since he doesn't fight; that there was nothing he could have taken from him, since he has nothing, desires nothing. He then takes El Topo's gun from him and shoots himself, then tells him, before dying in his arms, "You lost."

It is here, slightly more than halfway through the film, that El Topo's transformation can finally start to take place. He despairs entirely. Passing back through the destruction he has wrought, seeing the bodies he has left behind, he is congratulated by the woman for being the best, but rejects her admiration. It is only now, giving up on the goal of winning, of becoming the best and most feared, that El Topo places the masters he has already killed in the position of subjects-supposed-to-know. As we will see in the next section, he undergoes something like a complete subjective destitution, uttering a series of descriptions of the loss of his self before quoting Christ's last words on the cross in Golgotha, "My God, my God, why have you forsaken me?"

While in some ways *El Topo* is a film about the constant and repeated failure of transference—in that El Topo's resistances keep him from truly giving himself over to any subject-supposed-to-know—Jodorowsky's next film, *The Holy Mountain*, picks up from where *El Topo* left off by bringing into the picture a full-fledged subject-supposed-to-know almost right from the beginning. It is about a quarter of the way into a two-hour film when we meet the Alchemist, played by Jodorowsky, dressed all in white, at the end of a long rainbow-colored tunnel through which the thief has ventured. At first the thief attacks him, but the Alchemist, much like the last master in *El Topo*, deflects his knife thrusts with ease. He then pacifies the thief with a series of hand movements, and calls his assistant, a mostly nude woman with tattoos and sword-like fingernails, to come assist in a sort of shaman surgery. Holding the thief's hair up, the two reveal a tumor at the back of his neck. The Alchemist's assistant cuts into it, and a bright blue substance oozes out, after which the Alchemist pulls from the open tumor a slimy blue octopus-like creature.

Waking the thief from the trance he has been put into, the Alchemist then speaks his first words, asking him if he wants gold, to which the thief greedily nods. This is the point where the Alchemist has clearly established himself as the subject-supposed-to-know and something like transference takes effect. The thief follows all his instructions, including allowing himself to be baptized by the Alchemist and his assistant in an ornate pool with a pigmy hippo swimming in it, after which he is scoured clean (including his buttocks, in perhaps unnecessary cinematic detail) and led naked to a glass pot on the ground, into which the thief defecates. There follows a long process borrowing from a variety of traditions and rituals and involving something like a giant distillation machine with the poop in one glass vial and the thief sweating milk in the largest vial while a fire is stoked under him. At the end of this process the excrement has transformed into a lump of gold, which the Alchemist then hands to the thief, telling him, "You are excrement; you can transform yourself into gold." He then brings him a mirror, and the thief uses the block of gold to smash it, shattering his own mirror image.

The promise of gold, of a hidden treasure that the Alchemist's knowledge can help us find, and the faith kindled in the thief that trusting him is the way to achieving this treasure, is the key to the transference. The identification of the self with shit, and the destruction of the ego in the mirror, then becomes the next step, which we will explore in greater detail in the last chapter. The point to stress here is that Jodorowsky sees in ritual, in Tarot, and in religions a common power that can, if used well, be used to heal personal and social ills. As we discussed in the last chapter, after the episode with the thief, the Alchemist then gathers seven other followers, all wealthy captains of industry representing different planets and vices, becoming for each of them the subject-supposed-to-know. The trust they each decide to place in him opens the space for the transformations they undergo in the film's denouement.

To touch on one more example of the power of transference, let's turn again to *Santa Sangre*. As you will recall, in that film the protagonist, Fenix, has succumbed to his traumatic childhood and ended up in a mental asylum where he believes he is a bird of prey.

After a visit from his armless mother, he escapes the prison and begins to live with her, performing as her arms on stage and, at night, murdering young women who have tempted him sexually. During the first half of the film, the long flashback into Fenix's childhood, we meet a fellow child circus performer, Alma, who is a mime, her face always painted white, who is also deaf and mute. We first see Alma (the name means soul in Spanish) as she stands on a highwire platform. Her foster mother, the tattooed lady, has just lit the rope on fire and is demanding that she cross it, but Alma is afraid. The tattooed lady screams at her not to be afraid while striking the rope with a riding whip, and tells her to "read my lips, you stupid deaf-mute! I should have left you in the poorhouse when your mother died. Now practice!"

The relationship that develops between the young magician who sees his father seduced and ultimately betraying his lunatic mother and the deaf-mute girl who has lost her own mother and is caught in an abusive relationship with her replacement is deeply touching and provides the moral centerpiece to a movie that several commentators have noted precisely for its unusual morality, given the genre it represents. As the famed critique Robert Ebert wrote of it, it is "a horror film, one of the greatest, and after waiting patiently through countless Dead Teenager Movies, I am reminded by Alejandro Jodorowsky that true psychic horror is possible on the screen—horror, poetry, surrealism, psychological pain, and wicked humor, all at once."[31] The Rotten Tomatoes site calls it a "provocative psychedelic journey featuring the director's signature touches of violence, vulgarity, and an oddly personal moral center."[32] That oddly personal moral center emerges precisely in the relationship between the two young protagonists. And it is far from a coincidence, theoretically speaking, that Alma is a deaf-mute. Here I think we should avoid the obvious reading that the woman must be deprived of her voice in order for the male protagonist to find his. Rather, it seems that what is at stake here is precisely something like an analytic relationship, transference.

Fenix clearly loves Alma, and she loves him back. When she fears to walk the wire and balks at her stepmother's violent demands, she loses all fear and does it after an encounter with Fenix, in which he mimes a magic trick for her and produces out of thin air a cherry, which he gives to her. It is also not a coincidence that this key scene takes place in juxtaposition with the lascivious seduction scene between the tattooed lady and Fenix's father. While this relationship is all about the extremes of sexualized gender and power stereotypes, with the tattooed lady oozing desire as the knife-thrower plants blades closer and closer to the final phallic stab between her thighs, Fenix's and Alma's relationship is closer to the love relation as described by Lacan, in which each party gives the other what he or she does not have. Moreover, the very silence of Alma ultimately has a role in releasing Fenix from his deadly symptom, as we will see in greater detail in the next section.

Ultimately, though, the function of Alma's character is to starkly contrast with the role played by Fenix's mother. Where his mother roughly takes the place of the missing paternal function of fixing the flowing signifiers in Fenix's psychotic mental structure, thus filling him with the certainty of his place and role—he is to be her arms and hands, he is "nothing without her"—Alma replaces that certainty with silence, slowly moving his certain knowledge of his role to a hysterical question asked of the other: "who am I and what do you want of me?" Silent, like the analyst's presence behind a patient's divan, Alma patiently waits until Fenix's delusion breaks.[33]

Transference is the key to breaking out of the symptomatic suffering these characters and patience are trapped in, but transference can be abused. It can be used to lead subjects into ever further subjection. Any thrall to a religion or cult has transference-like characteristics. The difference, then, must lie in what one does with transference, who induces it, and how one acts once transference is established. This is where the third movement of the meaning cure—and the third section of this book—comes in. As we will see in what follows, this next crucial step cannot involve replacing a master signifier with another. The trust the patient, or the consumer of an artistic product, or the character in one of Jodorowsky's stories, places in the subject-supposed-to-know must, in some paradoxical sense, be betrayed or disappointed in order to be fulfilled. The subject-supposed-to-know cannot in fact know.

It is worth underlining this paradox a bit more, since in some ways the message of this chapter, that transference must be established for the cure to be effective, and the theme of the next, that transference must be destroyed for the cure to be effective, would seem to contradict each other. Indeed it seems self-defeating, unnecessary, and yet the point of psychoanalysis is that, in a profound way it is necessary to err, to momentarily project a falsehood onto the analyst that you later retract. Hence the title of Lacan's Seminar XXI: *Les Non-Dupes Errent*, a homophonic rendering of *les noms du père*, the names of the father, whose meaning translates roughly as, those who think they have avoided being duped are the ones making the gravest error.

For all his or her power in enabling the transference, in the end the subject-supposed-to-know must reveal himself or herself to be an idiot, or at the very least a catalyst for the subject's own discovery, the subject's own progression. And ultimately, to be truly effective, something altogether more profound must take place; namely, the subject must pass through a kind of symbolic death to be reborn as its authentic self. What that process involves, and what that authenticity might actually entail, is the subject of what follows.

4

Subjective Destitution

As we saw in our analysis of *Fando y Lis*, Fando's alternating between fawning care and raining abuse on Lis seems to relate to his own traumatic fixations around gender identity, separation from his mother, and death. Several scenes explicitly involve graves or imply them. In one, Fando and Lis come upon a hellish mud pit teeming with writhing, naked bodies, their features entirely obscured by the slime they roll about in. Fando urges Lis to submerge herself in it, while Lis resists in repulsion. In another, pivotal scene right before the "third act," Fando recreates the death of his mother, leading a quite obviously living woman from a makeshift hospital bed to a freshly dug grave, embracing her while she thanks him for destroying her, and then placing her in the hole and covering her with dirt as she repeats her grateful words of thanks. Right before he finishes the job, she calls out to him, and her hand rises above the grave to give him something. He takes it from her, and places it on the ground, where a bird quickly takes flight. The card that then appears to mark the end of the second act and beginning of the final act reads: "and when I tried to separate myself from her, I realized that we formed a single body with two heads."[1]

The third act then culminates in Fando's last desperate attempt to climb the mountain and attain the goal of Tar. Unable to do so, he lashes out in fury at Lis, eventually stoning her to death, at which point an enormous crowd appears and carries her to a coffin where they proceed to feast on her. The Christological trope then becomes all the sharper as Fando pulls her body from the coffin and bears it like a cross on his shoulders the rest of the way up the mountain. There he places Lis's body in a fresh grave, covered in white stone and lies down next to it, murmuring "Speak to me, Lis, speak to me," over and over. As the ground brush grows over his body, Lis rises naked and fresh from the grave like a newborn Eve. Across from her, another Fando, also naked and clean, stands in a clearing in the woods. Hand in hand they escape together into the forest, as the final card appears, reading: "when their image was erased from the mirror, on the glass appeared the word freedom."

Just as with the violent rending of bodies, relationships, and reality itself that constitute the film's trajectory, its end begs for a Lacanian clarification. As we saw, for Lacan the ego, what many other schools of psychotherapy consider their end and purpose to defend and strengthen, is merely the subject's most fundamental defense mechanism against the incoherence and radical contingency that threaten its sense of power and control over the world. Because the shell of the ego bakes into the subject's psychic life the very symptoms that cause the subject (and indeed the social body) to suffer—especially its enslavement to certain norms, such as gender roles and expectations, that perpetuate impossible-because-contradictory models of embodiment and behavior (for woman, purity and desirability; for man, stoic loyalty and unlimited sexual prowess)—the analytic

SUBJECTIVE DESTITUTION

process requires not its strengthening but its (at least temporary) dissolution, a process called subjective destitution. As Žižek puts it, "the psychoanalytic cure is effectively over when the subject loses this fear and freely assumes his own nonexistence."[2] It is only by passing through the fundamental fantasy upholding the ego's coherence and claim to power that something like freedom can be attained. But that freedom comes at a high cost, namely, abandoning the precious image of oneself that has accreted over a lifetime.

If the violence of desire ripples through all of Jodorowsky's filmic work and permeates the symptoms of the patients he endeavors to treat with psychomagic, and if something akin to transference appears to be a necessary mediator in those actions as well as in the narrative flow of his films, the dissolution of the subject and transcendence to a new, authentic sphere of being is yet again a common theme, both as the aim of his psychomagical cures as well as the moral center of his otherwise profligately violent films. Indeed, if a sort of subjective destitution is clearly at work in the denouement of *Fando y Lis*, we get a clearer exposition of how the installation of transference and the subject-supposed-to-know is followed by a process of subjective destitution in later installments of Jodorowsky's journey. And as we saw with our earlier discussions, there seems to be a kind of progression in the filmic work, as Jodorowsky himself starts to clarify how something like a method can arise from his own surrealist madness.

Fando y Lis is almost entirely a film about failure, the impossibility of the sexual relation, to put it in Lacanian terms, and the desperate, often misogynist violence that erupts from the desire to realize that impossible relation. In this light the transfiguration at the end of the film is surprising, even troubling. What motivates this newly emerged, Edenic couple? Has Fando not just stoned his lover to death? As with later Jodorowsky films, there is a sacrificial logic here, and Lis has clearly been placed, against her will, in the role of the *bouc émissaire*. Recall from our earlier discussion of René Girard's theory of the scapegoat that in its more atavistic cultural manifestations the animal sent to the sacrifice is actually conceived of by the polis as guilty, as in some ways responsible for the ills that have befallen the community, and hence its sacrifice will in some literal sense expiate those ills and cleanse the society. This is the stage where we find ourselves in the instance of Lis's violent sacrifice in *Fando y Lis*. Fando, exemplifying the misogynist fantasies according to which women hold the core to men's desired wholeness in the impossible construct of virginal purity and lascivious desire, deposits his perverse fantasies into Lis's body, believing they are actually hers, and then slaughters her in a kind of repetition of the age-old atrocity called the honor killing. The transition to the next phase in Girard's understanding begins only then, as Christological imagery emerges around Lis's resurrection from the grave. But in almost all senses and within the diegetic logic, the transformation from outright violence to redemption is in some ways unearned. Fando is the perpetrator, not the victim. And Lis in no way takes the sacrificial role on consciously or willingly.

It would seem to be the role of *El Topo* to undertake the next phase in Jodorowsky's analytic trajectory; and yet, here again we run into a kind of blockage, one that is fruitful to explore in some detail. As we have gone over in some detail, a little more than halfway through the film, El Topo has defeated three of the four masters, and the fourth has taken his own life. This leads to a kind of crisis of faith for the

SUBJECTIVE DESTITUTION

gunslinger, who screams in despair and retraces his journey past the bodies of his victims and to the woman, whose embrace and desire he rejects. Thus rejected, the woman turns to her lesbian lover, and the two take turns shooting El Topo, who has willingly dropped his gun and offered himself up in sacrifice. As noted before, the moment is fully Christological, replete with stigmata and Christ's last words on Golgotha, "My God, my God, why have you abandoned me?" Here then, the violence of desire again leads to a scapegoat, but with the important added step that El Topo appears to willingly take on this role. Nevertheless, *El Topo* is still a film about a failure of process. Or better said, where *Fando y Lis* points to the outcome of a process but fails to address the process itself (such that the transcendent denouement appears unmotivated, just another fantasy laid over the wasteland of gendered violence), in *El Topo* we have the necessary steps in place, but no transcendence. Despite assuming the sacrifice, himself, El Topo's journey still leads to bloody annihilation.

Nonetheless, in the middle of the film the idea of sacrifice leading to some kind of rebirth would seem to earn a literal mise-en-scene. Shortly after being shot up and left for dead by his former consorts, El Topo is discovered by a group of outcasts, mostly Native American, all destitute, and many handicapped or in some way disabled. This marks one of the most notable cases of Jodorowsky's passion for filling his films with people whose bodies are not often seen on screen and who, as a result of their physical appearance, are often shunned or looked askance at. It is certainly possible to ask if his repetitive use of disabled bodies in his films is in any way exploitative, in the way circus "freak shows" were. Indeed, Jodorowsky's own descent from circus workers and love of the circus adds urgency to that question. In his own telling

136 ALEJANDRO JODOROWSKY: FILMMAKER AND PHILOSOPHER

Jodorowsky has insisted that he shows disabled and non-normal bodies so frequently in his films because "he finds all bodies beautiful." To my mind, however, there is a deeper, even philosophical import to this emphasis on disability and disfigurement in his cinematic work, one that fits perfectly into the theme of this chapter.

One of the most damaging myths that the ego can and often does buy into as it develops is the idea that there is an ideal way to be that it must strive for. In Freud's own analysis of the structure of the ego, he identified precisely this split in the two terms he called the *ideal ego* and the *ego-ideal*. In some ways the self is splayed out, even drawn and quartered between these points of reference as it develops: on the one hand, an ideal ego that it imagines itself to be, but that is alienated, only produced via a mirror, originally, or other forms of mediation later in life; and on the other hand, an ego-ideal representing how the subject imagines being seen from the vantage of an ideal, perfect perspective, as if submitted to the judgment of a god. Jodorowsky's embrace of and obvious love for people with bodies that have, in the past, been destined for freakshows or, in the present, are marginalized, discarded, or ignored, should be seen as an attempt to strike against the iniquitous power of the ego-ideal, which inscribes itself in the form of an implicit knowledge of *how bodies ought to be*, a real existing standard out there in the world that we all approximate and likewise fall short of, each in different ways and to differing degrees. Rather than bodies to look down on or laugh at, Jodorowsky's disabled bodies are reminders that humans in all their glorious diversity are the real and only standard, and that any ego-ideal is nothing other than an imaginary projection beyond the reality of our shared partiality. We are, in other words, equal in being partial, fallen, and profoundly lacking—in a word, disabled. Disability is normal; the very presumption of normalcy inherent in ableism of any kind is itself the disease, the cause of socially imposed suffering.

In the context of *El Topo*, then, the moment of transition for El Topo arrives when he ceases on his journey to become the best—a journey clearly modeled on the ego-ideal of the ultimate black-leather-clad gunslinger and abetted by the gaze of the woman and her constant urging for him to become the best and defeat the masters—and lays down his gun, thus submitting himself to the role of sacrificial scapegoat with all its Christological symbolism. Left to die he is gathered up by the ragtag band of disabled bodies, who lay him on a bier of branches and drag him to their cave, while a voiceover intones "Show me your way and your paths. Show me the way of your truth. For you are the God of my salvation and I waited for you. You will show your sinners the way. You will put the humble on the path of justice." The film then shows a card with the title *Psalms*, and the next shot reveals Jodorowsky totally transformed. No longer wearing black but now mostly naked but for a white sari and sandals, his hair and beard bleached almost white, seated cross-legged high in a cave, bathed in luminescence.

Soon he is approached by a female dwarf who climbs a ladder to reach him and proceeds to apply make-up to his face, then caresses his body and kisses him on the mouth, at which point he appears to wake with a start. Coming down from his perch he confronts the woman and tells her he is not a god, but a man, and asks how long he has been there, to which she responds, since before her birth. She tells him that she has always taken care of him, and that the old woman tells them that he will liberate them. She then takes him through the enormous cave where her people, all in poverty, exhibiting various forms of disfigurement or disability, live in barrels stacked high upon one another. She then explains that they have been prisoners here for many years, and that the only escape is through a hole high in the cave ceiling, which they cannot reach. She then takes him to the old woman, whose lead El Topo follows in sucking from the body of a desiccated beetle, thus consuming a powerful hallucinogenic drug under whose sway he undergoes precisely the kind of rebirth rituals we have seen Jodorowsky stage for his patients, this time emerging from beneath the old woman as if a newly born child.

The newborn "prophet" then has his head shorn and dons the attire of a monk, at which point he announces to his "people" his plan: to dig a tunnel to connect the cave with the village outside. To undertake the plan, he needs funds to buy dynamite, so he takes on various demeaning jobs in the nearby village, a den of bourgeois iniquity and religious fanaticism. In the end his new manifestation as a peaceful monk ends up no more successful than his previous life as a gunslinger, and in a display of superhuman strength he destroys the village in retribution for their massacre of his people before dousing himself with gasoline and lighting himself on fire, in obvious reference to the self-immolation of Thích Quảng Đức, the Vietnamese Buddhist monk who burned himself to death in 1963 in protest of the South Vietnamese government's persecution of Buddhists.

The clear and present question then becomes, why does *El Topo* become, in effect, a tale of two failures? Why after what is evidently a self-sacrifice and rebirth in a new pacifist version as a kind of monk-like figure, does Jodorowsky have El Topo again fail, and again fall into the cycle of death and violence that characterized him as a gunslinger?

The answer seems to lie in the religious overtones of the moment of his conversion. Recall that during his "death" the gunslinger narrates in voiceover a series of Biblical lines, including Christ's last words from Golgotha. But it turns out that many of the lines in Jodorowsky's voiceover come from the same Psalm quoted by Christ at the moment of his death as reported in the Gospels of both Matthew and Mark—Psalm 22, which recounts the plaints of a pious man to God, a man who suffers from the nearness of death, who is "poured out like water," his bones "out of joint," who has been laid "in the dust of death," who is encircled by evildoers who "have pierced my hands and feet." The following voiceover, in turn, as El Topo is dragged away to his new home, comes from Psalm 25.

The transition, in other words, is marked by a distinct move from one series of masters, the earthly gunslinging variety, to another, the religious master, the teacher of dogmas and faith. While El Topo does try to disavow being treated as a god, it appears he cannot avoid the typecasting, for his very performance of humility and poverty ends up recreating the godlike demeanor of prophets from Christ to such monks as Thich Quang Duc. In other words, what *El Topo* seems to be exploring is the very problematic of the promise of redemption as conveyed by any kind of master discourse. It matters little, Jodorowsky implies, whether the master in question is profane and explicitly violent or, at the other extreme, outwardly pacificist as Christ was—if the kind of belief deposited on that leader, on that subject-supposed-to-know, is structured like a discourse of mastery. In such cases the violence of our desire for redemption, for wholeness, inevitably takes over and the results can only be further suffering, further bloodshed. How else to explain the perversion of an entire religious philosophy founded on the principles of self-sacrifice, abnegation, altruism, and pacifism, leading to the kind of internecine violence and destruction, hatred, and discrimination that Christianity has managed to partake in during the 2000 years of its existence? You are searching for a new master, El Topo seems to be telling us, and you will find one.

That said, if *Fando y Lis* lacked a mechanism for potentially leaving behind the violence of desire and instead gestured toward a redemption it could not realize, *El Topo* instead shows the mechanism, transference, but only reveals its dangers, not its possibilities. That will be left to the films to follow and to the practice that Jodorowsky eventually develops some ten years later. The mechanism in question, one gestured to but never fully developed in *El Topo*, is nothing other than subjective destitution, the process whereby the subject finally lets go of the fundamental fantasy that has soldered its ego around an impossible and self-contradictory object of desire and passes through that fantasy to embrace the drive animating it. To better understand the nature of this movement and the potential liberation it offers for the subject, it makes sense to spell out in greater detail the distinction between desire and drive in Lacan's thought, especially since he himself didn't really work out this distinction until relatively well into his trajectory as a teacher.

Slavoj Žižek points out this shift in Lacan's thought and also makes it responsible for a prevalent misreading of the very notion of the cure in Lacanian psychoanalysis. The prevalent misreading suggests that the cure involved coming to terms with the ultimate impossibility of attaining a full jouissance that the subject unconsciously assumes was once there but was lost through the advent of language and symbolic castration. This notion of the cure, easily available on a reading of

Lacan's thought through the 1950s, amounts to identifying it with *subjectivization*, namely, the subject stops living inauthentically, in bad faith, as it were, stops covering the gaping lack at its core with fantasies of fulfillment and instead accepts the fundamental, constitutive nature of the lack at its core. In Žižek's words, "'Subjectivization' thus consists in the purely formal gesture of symbolic conversion, by means of which the subject integrates into his symbolic universe—turns into part and parcel of his life-narrative, provides with meaning—the meaningless contingency of his destiny."[3]

To this version of the cure Žižek contrasts the idea of subjective destitution, which emerges in the 1960s and 1970s, which he described as such:

> In clear contrast to "subjectivization," "subjective destitution" involves the opposite gesture: at the end of the psychoanalytic cure, the analysand has to suspend the urge to symbolize/internalize, to interpret, to search for a "deeper meaning"; he has to accept that the traumatic encounters which traced out the itinerary of his life were utterly contingent and indifferent, that they bear no "deeper message."

While I'm not sure we need to go as far as calling it an opposite message, the point to take here is how the role of interpretation and the promise of a further or final interpretation implicit in the earlier version of the cure carries the risk of repeating the very gestures that kept the subject vacillating in its prior repetition compulsions, clinging to a new answer around the next bend. In other words, the very interpretation offered by the subject-supposed-to-know could itself continue to function as an *objet petit a*, thus flummoxing the

142 ALEJANDRO JODOROWSKY: FILMMAKER AND PHILOSOPHER

shift from desire to drive that Lacan would later describe as the goal of the cure.

As Žižek goes on to explain, the reason for both the misreading and why the subjectivization paradigm is in fact faulty are the same: they both fail to consider the fact that the insertion of the symbolic order into the subject's lived experience not only creates the hole of lack at its core, but that it also at the same time produces jouissance. Jouissance, in other words, is not truly lost; the emergence of a signifier carrying with it the presence and absence of a now desired object infuses the negative space of the object's disappearance with jouissance. Jouissance flows from the very oscillation of opposites, the very dialectic of desire that impels the subject toward its destructive urges. If the ego then builds itself up as a protective armor against the traumatic presence of this kernel, it does so by abjuring the draw of that jouissance, by repressing it, disavowing it, or in the case of psychotics, foreclosing entirely the representative functions of language that produce it.

The misreading in the early version of the cure is based on something like a missed step in the process whereby a physical, non-linguistic infant becomes a symbolically mediated, castrated subject. This step only comes into view when Lacan starts to differentiate desire, on the one hand, and physical needs or animal instincts on the other, from something altogether different, which he derives from Freud's theory: drive. On the one hand, unlike desire, drive doesn't postpone, push ahead of it, some promise of jouissance. Rather, drive pulsates with jouissance, repetitively circling the objects it has infused with it. And unlike desire, this jouissance comes from the very failure to attain the object of desire. It draws from desire's reserves, as it were, and reappropriates that jouissance into something finally satisfying. On the other hand, unlike physical needs and instincts, drives are specifically human; they are the result, the potent byproducts, of human animals learning to navigate the world through language. As Žižek writes,

> Lacan's point here is that the passage from the radically "impossible" Real (the maternal Thing-Body which can be apprehended only in a negative way) to the reign of the symbolic Law, to desire which is regulated by Law, sustained by the fundamental Prohibition, is not direct: something happens between the "pure," "pre-human" nature and the order of symbolic exchanges, and this "something" is precisely the Real of drives—no longer the "closed circuit" of instincts and of their innate rhythm of satisfaction (drives are already "derailed nature"), but not yet the symbolic desire sustained by Prohibition. The Lacanian Thing is not simply the "impossible" Real which withdraws into the dim recesses of the Unattainable with the entry of the symbolic order; it is the very universe of drives.[4]

Thus when the later interpretation of the cure in Lacanian analysis figures it as a piercing of the fundamental fantasy and a passage from desire to drive, what is at stake is not merely an acceptance at an intellectual level of the radical contingency of one's life, for example, although it certainly includes that. More radically, more to the point, the subject must learn to replace the endless deferral inherent in desire with a kind of satisfaction with the partial drives that constitute his or her particular way of inhabiting the world.

The key here, as Žižek goes on to emphasize, is that the unconscious, structured like a language as Lacan never ceased to

144 ALEJANDRO JODOROWSKY: FILMMAKER AND PHILOSOPHER

teach, is not, as is almost universally understood even in Freudian circles, what is left behind, hidden beneath the surface as language and reason enter the subject in the form of a rational ego; rather the unconscious *is* the manifestation of reason in the subject, it is the very working of language with all its slippages, faults, and combinations, as it goes about following its logical imperatives without the guidance of the self's constraints in a physical reality. As this disembodied logic impresses itself on the meat of the human animal, the mortification of that flesh by its relentless churning creates an undercurrent of madness, which is beautifully captured in this famous quote from Hegel:

> The human being is this night, this empty nothing, that contains everything in its simplicity—an unending wealth of many representations, images, of which none belongs to him—or which are not present. This night, the inner of nature, that exists here— pure self—in phantasmagorical representations, is night all around it, in which here shoots a bloody head, there another white ghastly apparition, suddenly here before it, and just so disappears. One catches sight of this night when one looks human beings in the eye—into a night that becomes awful.[5]

This night of the world with its phantasmatic cornucopia is the kernel of ourselves that we encounter ever so briefly in dreams; in slippages of the tongue; in the jokes that suddenly make us roar in laughter; or in the weird and embarrassing ways we find all too specific objects, people, body parts, or situations to be arousing. And this night of the world is, naturally, what the surrealists explore with every ounce of their creative abilities. Finally, it is this night of the world that has been put aside or covered over for the ego to enter into polite society; and it is this night of the world which must be reawakened if, as is so often the case, that ego must be torn down and rebuilt, because it has been constructed in ways that bake into it unbearable symptoms.

The socially acceptable ego is in some ways a specifically aesthetic construct. If you think about how carefully we go about dressing, behaving, caring for our bodies, or, even if we don't, staging our very disregard for such norms in ways that are themselves in turn acceptable under alternative norms, you quickly see that the construction of the ego is often and normatively about foregrounding the beautiful and hiding the ugly. The symbolization of the real and the creation of the ego's polite society, in other words, is at another level the designation of the real as something ugly that needs to be covered, removed from that polite society:

> Contrary to the standard idealist argument which conceives ugliness as the defective mode of beauty, as its distortion, one should assert the ontological primacy of ugliness: it is beauty which is a kind of defense against the Ugly in its repulsive existence or, rather, existence tout court, since ... what is ugly is ultimately the brutal fact of existence (of the real) as such.[6]

And here, at the nexus between the night of the world and the ugly, we can see some of the sources of Jodorowsky's fascinations with, for example, people with abject and rejected bodies, whose disability has condemned them to being excluded by polite society, put into colonies away from the public, whose eyes avoid them because their deformity offends. We can also see why, as part of his practice as well as in the process he depicts in his films, the path to enlightenment passes through a phase that we could call with Hegel the night of the world.

Indeed, this is exactly what we see occur when Jodorowsky's trajectory finally matures in *The Holy Mountain*. Recall that in the scene discussed in the second section above, the alchemist asks the thief if he wants gold. When the thief replies he does, the alchemist has him defecate in a clear bowl, and then initiates an elaborate ritual whereby we see the thief's excrement transformed into a lump of gold, at which point the alchemist tells him, "You are excrement. You can change yourself into gold." He then shows the thief a mirror, and the thief immediately smashes his image with the lump of gold.

While far from the film's denouement, two central themes enter in this scene. The first is the identification of the thief's sense of self with both gold and shit. The thief's journey so far has been motivated in part by material gain. His participation in the circus of toads and chameleons is for paying tourists; his likeness to Jesus is also monetized; indeed, his climbing of the tower is inspired by a desire to find gold there. But more profoundly, perhaps, the thief engages with the alchemist in the hopes of finding gold in himself. The precious core of oneself—what Lacan referred to as *agalma* in reference to Alcibiades's term for the fascinating source of Socrates's charisma, "something beyond all good,"[7] that led him and others to be seduced by the philosopher—is instrumental in producing the transference. In this sense it is a precise correlate to the *subject-supposed-to-know*. The thief, like the analysand, begins by projecting into the person of the alchemist a kind of wisdom and knowledge about the thief's self. You are excrement, but you can change yourself into gold, is thus both the promise of the guru/analyst, but also the secret to his

SUBJECTIVE DESTITUTION

method. This love, Lacan says, is "essentially a deception." In locating agalma in him or herself, the analyst triggers the transference and also triggers the emergence of the analysand's fundamental fantasy, "centered on the ideal point ... placed somewhere in the Other, from which the Other sees me, in the form I like to be seen." The paradox of this central point—that it is something one desires in the other and at the same time a place from which one imagines being seen in an ideal form—engenders a primordial aggression, in which the subject essentially says "I love you, but because I love something in you more than you—the *objet petit a*—I mutilate you." This then is the source of the surrealists' fragmented bodies, their mortified imaginary landscapes. Descending a level below the slick coherence of social reality, they discover a landscaped shredded by desire, pockmarked by the *objet petit a*, Buñuel's *Obscure Object of Desire* that leads us from one errant and ephemeral satisfaction to the next, in desperate search of something *that is not that.*

Assuming the position of the agalma in the relationship with the analysand is necessary but insufficient in the cure. What comes next is the kicker. For the way to wisdom and self-knowledge to be opened, the analysand must come to the realization that that the longed for agalma is "a gift of shit."[8] Jodorowsky's surrealist expression is a direct recognition of the proximity of violence and enlightenment, and of the role art and therapy have in preventing the "*psychotic passage à l'acte*" precisely by staging the emergence of the fundamental fantasy in art or in the transference and not in the space of social reality.

To avoid both eruptions of ego-protecting violence and full psychotic meltdown, Lacan taught that the subject needs to use the transference to come to grip with and expose to the analyst his or her most intimate, awful, and mortifying desires; to own them, as it were. In so doing, the subject comes to the realization that "the story I have been telling myself about myself no longer makes sense" and, at least for a brief spell, "I no longer have a self to make sense of."[9]

We see this stage in full bloom during the final conflagrations of *Holy Mountain*. The industrialists join the alchemist and the thief on their journey, which requires that they first burn all their money, and then burn in effigy wax figures of themselves. Their trek to the top of the Holy Mountain requires them to undergo a series of trials, culminating in ecstatic visions of their worst fears: visions of themselves eating the flesh of living animals; taking part in animal copulation; being castrated and hung on a tree filled with chicken carcasses; being covered in tarantulas; sucking milk from the sagging breast of an ancient androgynous person whose breasts then turn to jaguar heads—Jodorowsky's ultimate cinematic exploration of Hegel's night of the world.

At the end of their journey, the industrialists gather around a table with the alchemist, who reveals to them that he is the film director Alejandro Jodorowsky. "We came in search of the secret of immortality," he tells them, "to be like gods. And here we are, more human than ever." Then he continues, "If we have not attained immortality, at least we have attained reality. We began in a fairy tale, and we came to life. But is this life reality? No, it is a film. Zoom back camera." As the camera recedes to reveal a film set, Jodorowsky stands up and bids his fellow actors to accompany him, "We shall not stay here, prisoners," he insists to them, "we shall break the illusion." And then he intones, "Goodbye to the Holy Mountain. Real life awaits us," as they take their leave of the set, and the film fades to white.

In the therapeutic practice he developed, which mixes aspects from his early fascinations with Tarot, radical theater, surrealism, and a variety of psychoanalytic and philosophical influences, Jodorowsky recreates similar pathways in order to lead his patients "to make peace with [their] subconscious, not becoming independent of it but making it an ally."[10] The mechanism he uses to help them come to this new relation with their unconscious is remarkably similar to the transference as Lacan described it, although, again, the speed with which it purportedly occurs would seem surprising to most psychoanalysts. Indeed, his use of the term "subconscious" instead of the psychoanalytically accepted "unconscious" is telling in that regard, suggestive of how the psychomagic patients don't seem to need long intake periods where they figure out what is wrong with them; rather they seem to know what's wrong as soon as they come in the door. It's as if their problems were subconscious or preconscious to begin with, rather than genuinely unconscious and in need of years of poking and prodding in order to be made manifest in daylight reality. And yet, the process remains profoundly similar. In Jodorowsky's telling, "I became a screen on which" his patients could "vent their bottled up hatred."[11] To become that screen, the psychomagicians present themselves "only as a technical expert, as an instructor," and explain to the patients "the symbolic meaning and purpose of every act."[12] This is in contrast to the patients' expectations of a guru, a popular charlatan who "must present himself as a superior being who knows all mysteries."[13]

In this sense, his patients follow the path exposited both by *The Holy Mountain* and by the psychoanalytic transference. We, the thief, the analysand, turn the alchemist or the analyst into the

150 ALEJANDRO JODOROWSKY: FILMMAKER AND PHILOSOPHER

subject-supposed-to-know. We deposit there our agalma, that which is in us more than us. Its proximity to our social reality causes that reality to give way; the grotesqueries of our deepest fears and desires come to the surface. And then the alchemist shows us his cards. He was never in control, never had access to agalma. We must face life on its own terms, freed from our ego's carefully constructed prison, yes, but also exposed to all the uncertainties and banalities that existence holds in store.

According to Žižek, in passing through the fundamental fantasy and choosing the level of drive over that of desire, "the subject in an unheard-of way, 'causes itself,' becomes its own cause: its cause is no longer decentered, i.e. the enigma of the Other's desire no longer has any hold over it." As he goes on to write:

> [B]y way of positing itself as its own cause, the subject fully assumes the fact that the object-cause of its desire is not a cause which precedes its effects but is retroactively posited by the network of its effects: an event is never simply in itself traumatic, it only becomes a trauma retroactively, by being "secreted" from the subject's symbolic space as its inassimilable point of reference.[14]

This is because, as we have seen, in entering into language and organizing its libidinal life according to the structural modes of a language, the subject's objects of desire are situated as such by the role of metaphor, the temporal stopgaps that emerge and establish the meaning of a given sentence, story, or configuration retroactively, as that which must have always been the case. At the same time, one of the basic functions of the symbolic order is to "naturalize" that process, to make it seem as though the meanings we necessarily produce ourselves were already there, awaiting our discovery—hence the retroactive causality is masked by our daily practices and beliefs.

This rendering objective of our self-produced meanings, as if they preceded us, entails a belief that the Other exists, that the Other is founded, justified, that nothing ultimately is contingent. Hence passing from desire, which is sustained by precisely this fundamental fantasy of the independent existence of the Other, to drive, itself entails the implosion of that belief—which is why drive in some profound way involves self-birth: in embracing one's own partial drives one stops passing the buck, one stops endowing some Other with the responsibility for the way one is and one identifies with one's own particular, pathological enjoyments.

But remember that the subject is sustained as subject precisely by its question to the Other, by its belief that the Other somehow does hold the secret to its being. Because of this, the radical move from desire to drive also requires short-circuiting that question and that dependence. In other words, by losing its belief in the Other's special knowledge, the subject is forced to confront its own self-production, which in turn requires a kind of destruction of the very status of subjectivity itself. Piercing the fantasy, replacing desire with drive, thus entails what Lacan calls subjective destitution.

As Žižek puts it:

The most elementary matrix of fantasy, of its temporal loop, is that of the "impossible" gaze by means of which the subject is present at the act of his/her own conception. What is at stake in it, is the enigma of the Other's desire: by means of the fantasy-formation, the subject provides an answer to "What am I for my parents, for their desire?" and thus endeavors to arrive at the "deeper meaning" of his or her existence, to discern the Fate involved in it.[15]

And here we have the explanation for the particular efficacy of Jodorowsky's various actions and scenarios involving the "birth" of fully formed adults, whether in the psychomagical actions designed for the young woman who feared being pregnant or the married couple who had lost their way, or in the pivotal scene in *El Topo* where he is reborn under the hallucinogenic guidance of the old woman. In each of these cases what Jodorowsky's move suggests is a literal enactment of self-birthing. *Do not ask any longer what your parents desired when you were born; it is irrelevant. You are born when you yourself learn to will your own existence, under your own terms; and to do this you have to rid yourself of the fantasy that this knowledge precedes and awaits you.*

Importantly, the only way that this shift from desire to drive can take place, and what permits the subjective destitution that frees a subject from its enthrallment to the violence of the dialectic of desire, is the dissolution of the transference, the moment where the subject-supposed-to-know reveals that he or she knows nothing, was a simple spectator all along. We saw this move occur explicitly at the end of *The Holy Mountain*, when Jodorowsky orders the cameras to pull back and simply states that he is not the Alchemist but nothing other than a film director, and then he and the others engage in a long bout of absurd laughter before getting up and walking off into plain old reality. We also see it in *Santa Sangre*, albeit within the diegetic space of the fiction.

SUBJECTIVE DESTITUTION

In *Santa Sangre*, Fenix's symptom—in his case, where he has foreclosed the representative nature of the paternal function, a fully psychotic delusion concerning the continued existence in the real of his dead mother—the meaning of his existence has become fully fused with his mother's desire. He knows why he exists—because she tells him. He exists to complete her, to serve her as her arms and hands. Fenix's path to emerging from his murderous delusion involves first his love and hence transference for Clara, the mime-faced deaf-mute. Once out and free again as an adult after escaping the insane asylum, Fenix encounters a grown Alma, whom the tattooed lady is trafficking, selling her to disgusting drunk men with the promise that, since she is a deaf-mute, the men "can do whatever you want with her, and no one will hear her." In this particular event, Alma awakes to being held by a giant soldier, and starts silently kicking and screaming before managing to break a bottle on his head and escape through the window. As she hides under a blanket on top of a parked firetruck, her last vision before pulling the blanket over her head is of a shadow moving down the street toward the house she just escaped. We then start to occupy the POV of that shadow, as he moves into the den of iniquity that is the redlight district where Alma lives with her stepmother. As the POV approaches the tattooed lady's door, we cut to her inside, enraged that Alma has escaped, and now hearing the approach of someone she thinks is Alma. She jumps to her feet grabbing a riding crop with which to beat the girl, and we are again transported to the external POV, where we see a beautifully manicured hand push the door open, and the tattooed lady's expression changes from rage to horror. Now we see the hand again, this time releasing a throwing knife, which cuts through the

154   ALEJANDRO JODOROWSKY: FILMMAKER AND PHILOSOPHER

air, perfectly piercing the tattooed lady's belly. The same manicured hand then pulls the knife from her and stabs again and again, and the scene ends in a gratuitously comical allusion to the *Psycho* shower scene that inspires it: a view of the tattooed lady pressing up against what initially looks like a plastic shower curtain, before a close-up makes it clear that it is a translucent curtain, which her dying body then rips as she falls through it.

While we officially don't yet know this, the scene is the first encounter between the adult protagonists. Alma is still a traumatized victim of her foster mother; Fenix is in thrall to his hallucinated mother, having replaced the gaping absence of a foreclosed paternal metaphor with the presence "in the real" of the Other. In full psychoanalytic parlance, Fenix can only heal by undergoing a rebirth from the ashes of his own subjective destitution. To do this he must first become subjectivized, in other words, he must ask the question of what the Other wants of him, rather than knowing the answer with the certainty of a paranoid psychotic, and only then move from the desire for a final answer to the embrace of the radical contingency of his own embodied, driven self. Crucially, the partial satisfaction of the level of drive is not equivalent to the "enjoyment" of either the psychotic or, at a less extreme level, the pervert, both of whom either explicitly and consciously, in the case of the psychotic, or implicitly and unconsciously, in the case of the pervert, believe that the Other exists and that any enjoyment they are experiencing is done entirely for that Other. While these positions also entail a kind of subjective destitution, for them

[T]he big Other exists, while the subject at the end of the psychoanalytic process assumes the nonexistence of the big Other.

In short, the Other for whom the subject "makes herself ... (seen, heard, active)" has no independent existence and ultimately relies on the subject herself—in this precise sense, the subject who makes herself the Other's object-cause becomes her own cause.[16]

In order for Fenix to fully pass through the fantasy and truly become his own cause in this way, he must renew the transference he lost when his childhood was ripped from him. If his hallucinated mother has played the role of fully present *agalma*, his precious soul, what is in him more than himself, that must be replaced first by another soul, literally *alma* in Spanish. In opposition to his domineering dead mother, who cannot stop talking, Alma remains silent behind her painted face, an enigma who seems to promise a knowledge of himself he doesn't yet have.

When Alma sees posters for Fenix's performance as his mother she starts to investigate, and ultimately finds the ramshackle house he lives in. While we have until now only seen the house from the perspective of Fenix's delusion, through her eyes we finally see the house as it is, as a wreck, replete with a dummy of his mother in the hallways and, up in her haunted-house like bedroom, another one in her bed—something we only suspect at this point, though, since Alma raises the bedsheets to gaze on the body but doesn't reveal more than her own grimace. Indeed, rather than react in horror to what she has found with classical horror-film screams, Alma calmly moves to the dressing table, takes a tub of white makeup she finds there and starts to paint her face.

Meanwhile, Fenix—who has unsuccessfully tried to stymy the violence of his desire by bringing home an ostensibly female wrestler and urging her to fight him off when he then attacks her—is confronted by the hallucinatory revolt of his victims, dozens of white-painted women who rise from his backyard graveyard. As he reels inside to escape this nightmare vision, he runs into Alma, in the circus guise from their youth. The film immediately slows down, Fenix takes her hands and says, "Alma, I have been waiting for you for so long," and then they embrace and kiss. He then asks her if she has come to take him away, to which she silently nods. But there is one more obstacle to face. She guides him past the relics of his delusion toward his mother's bed, but before she can get there, his delusion manifests itself and his mother intervenes. Here we encounter the cinematic brilliance of Jodorowsky, which subtly shifts back and forth between the perspective of Alma, for which the house is an empty relic and there is no living mother, and Fenix, for whom his mother appears, demanding that he cut off the arms of, and thus kill, the girl who is trying to take her son away.

Fenix reacts as if in a trance, taking his knives and going toward Alma all the while struggling against himself. She in turn raises her arms and awaits him silently. The scene is interrupted by a woman with whom he had made a date walking in at just the wrong moment, to which he responds with a throwing knife hitting the doorjamb right by her head. When we return from her desperate flight out of the house to a telephone to call the police, Fenix is now in the usual position behind his mother, his arms replacing hers. But as they approach Alma, her arms still open wide, Fenix, now subjectivized by Alma's stance, split inside between the desire to fulfill his mother's wishes and his desire not to kill the woman he loves, turns the knife inward, slashing down at his mother's body.

As his mother and his other hallucinations one after another disappear, we are treated to flashbacks of the moment he is pulled from the trailer from which he watched the murder-suicide death of his parents so many years ago. Finally accepting that his mother is dead, Fenix follows Alma to the bed where, after clearing a flock of pigeons off her body, he pulls back the covers to reveal a ventriloquist dummy—at which point we flash back to scenes we have witnessed of him and his mother together, only this time seeing them for what they were: performances for his own sake using the dummy in place of his dead mother. He then destroys the dummy and proceeds to wreck the other altars and effigies throughout the house, finally freeing himself of the influence this embodied Other has played in his psychic life. As the effigies burn, Alma gently removes the fake nails from his hands, allowing him to reclaim his own responsibility for his hands as partial objects. They no longer serve another master; they are his to enjoy, his to own as well.

Indeed, this very point is hammered home in the last scene. Alma uses her hands to mime the bird tattooed on his chest flying away in an act of freedom. She then leads him outside to where the police are waiting. "Put your hands up," they shout. Fenix, looking down in wonder at his own hands, realizes they are his to control, and smiles in joy as he raises them to the sky, saying over and over again, "My hands, my hands, my hands." As the camera pulls back, Jodorowsky ends the film with a card bearing a quotation, again, from Psalms (143:6, 8): "I stretch out my hands to thee; my soul thirsts for thee like a parched land ... Teach me the way I should go, for to thee I lift up my soul." His hands in the air, Fenix isn't pleading to the police to save his life, he is exchanging the prior subject of his desire, his mother, for

158 ALEJANDRO JODOROWSKY: FILMMAKER AND PHILOSOPHER

an open question. Psalms 143 phrases the recipient of that question as God, of course. But in Jodorowsky's philosophy, such religious texts clearly point to a deeper underlying dynamic. Fenix's desire, his soul's thirst, won't be satisfied, won't be restored to any prior state of wholeness. Its only satisfaction lies in claiming his hands again for himself, for they and they alone can lift up his soul.

Jodorowsky's theme of destroying effigies of parents or, in some cases, sending them away on balloons, clearly finds its significance in the concept of subjective destitution. The idea here is that whether in "normal" neurotic mode or in more abnormal manifestations such as the one he imagines for Fenix, the patient has offloaded his own enjoyment as well as, crucially, the responsibility for that enjoyment, on some idea of the Other. By first identifying that Other with a parental image and then allowing the patient to destroy that image, Jodorowsky plays out the act of liberation whereby the patient finally takes ownership of his or her own enjoyment—I am not doing what I do for anyone else, ultimately it is for me, and I have to take responsibility for that. But also key to this process is something that emerges in Fenix's case and that ramifies in others as well: in destroying a parental image, the subject is also destroying and hence freeing himself or herself from a specific sense of self, one formed in response to that idea of the Other.

Perhaps the most dramatic example from his cinematic work appears in the first chapter of his autobiographical films, *The Dance of Reality*. This film principally deals with Jodorowsky's imagination of the life of his father, Jaime, a Jewish, Stalinist, atheist, and abusive circus-worker turned shop-owner. After a failed attempt to murder the Chilean dictator Ibáñez whom Jodorowsky visually

SUBJECTIVE DESTITUTION

associates with Nazis, Jaime loses his memory and disappears from the family for an extended period. The failure of his plot is due to Jaime's repressed admiration for the man, who, while representing the party politically opposed to Jaime's leftist leanings, ultimately embodies the very same overbearing idea of manhood that he aspired to and that he sees in Stalin.

After he finally returns to the family, Jaime now suffers from a paralysis in his hands, which are cramped into useless claws. His wife and Alejandro's mother, Sara, steps into the role of analyst and performs an action that leads to his eventual cure (albeit temporary, since he returns to his domineering and abusive ways for much of the second movie, *Endless Poetry*).

When Jaime protests that "nobody will be able to cure me," she replies, "you will cure yourself." To effect the cure she brings him into their backyard where she has put up on a bench a large portrait of Jaime's hero, Joseph Stalin. She then says, "look at your god," and goes toward the portrait, lifting it up to reveal another portrait below it, this time of Ibáñez, also in military garb, to which she then says (sings, since she always operatically sings her lines) "Look at the devil you admire. You found in Ibáñez all you admired in Stalin." Then, in a coup de grace, Sara removes Ibáñez's image to reveal another portrait below it, this one of Jaime himself, in a Stalinist jacket. "And here you are." She continues. "You are the same as they are! You have lived in the guise of a tyrant."

At this Jaime breaks down, wailing that he is so sorry, and Sara tells him that this man, the man who cries and feels, is his real self, the one they love as he is now, vulnerable and broken. She then hands Jaime a pistol. His cramped fingers slowly open to grasp it. He aims and fires at his own portrait, which bursts into flames along with those of the two dictators. After this climactic scene, the film cuts to young Alejandro and his two parents, Jaime now with his wild hair trimmed and his unruly beard shaven leaving his customary mustache, well dressed, and walking to the small port of Tocopilla. There they board a purple boat and sail away toward a new life in Santiago, as another version of Alejandro walks toward them through paper cutouts of the various figures we have met from his memories.

Panning back to the purple boat, we see the same actor now in the arms of the real, present-day Jodorowsky, with a man dressed as a skeleton behind them. As we watch them sail into the distance, Jodorowsky intones in voice over, "I felt the liftoff from the past land in an adult body, supporting the weight of painful years, but keeping the child in my heart." As the camera moves again from the boat to the distant dock back to the boat, now only Jodorowsky and the skeleton remain, and his VO continues, "like a living host, a white canary, like a worthy diamond, like a lucidity without walls, doors, and open windows through which the wind blows, only the wind, nothing but the wind."[17] And the purple boat fades into the fog and disappears entirely.

Clearly these culminating scenes from *Dance of Reality* lay out an approach to curing the subject of the pathologies wrought by a past full of suffering. As always there are three parts: an exposition of the suffering wrought by desire and an exploration of the events leading up to it; the positioning of a subject-supposed-to-know and the production of transference; and finally, the effecting of an action that stages a kind of traversal of the fantasy exposed by the transference. In this case, and primary to the film itself and the first part of the autobiography, the fantasy exposed is one whereby Jodorowsky's various traumas—his weakness as a child, his effeminacy, his love of poetry—are due to his father's violent, domineering nature. While no doubt containing truth, the fantasy ultimately acts as a support for the continuance of symptoms.

What *Dance of Reality* then focuses on is the subjective destitution required to recenter Jodorowsky's subjectivity away from its dependence on the desire of an Other, in this case that of his father. Jaime's destruction of the image of himself as tyrant, the tyrant of his own ego shaped in the image of powerful men he admires, even unconsciously, in order to recenter his own identity and take responsibility for his own jouissance, is precisely mirrored in a film in which Jodorowsky recenters his own identification away from his father. Thus, the final words of the film are, appropriately, lines of poetry, their meaning chiaroscuro, in part clearly referencing the child he carries in his memories and identifying that remembered child as the lucidity without walls but with open doors and windows through which the wind can blow. A self, not caged by ego and expectations, but open to contingency, to the wiles of various interpretations, and to the shattering eruptions of poetry in everyday life.

In some ways it is necessary to watch the final scene of *Dance of Reality* almost as if superimposed on the final scene of *Endless Poetry*—indeed, the two are made as if in echo of one another. As *Endless Poetry* comes to an end, a now adult but still young Alejandro walks to the end of a dock much like the one he left from Tocopilla, but this one in Santiago, carrying nothing but a suitcase. His father (and recall, Jodorowsky uses his own sons as actors in his films, so this role is played by his older son Brontis) runs to

162 ALEJANDRO JODOROWSKY: FILMMAKER AND PHILOSOPHER

catch up with him, and berates him for leaving Chile without telling him. Then he mocks his idea of emigrating to France, reminding him that he doesn't speak a word of French and asking him if he plans on living from his "little poems" (*poemitas*). Alejandro then lashes out at him, saying "You're no father! You never hugged me or spoke affectionately!" Jaime answers with homophobic slurs, and the two come to blows on the dock, the windy Pacific Ocean at their backs. Alejandro wins the battle, wrestling his father to the ground and kicking him several times in the side. He then turns away from Jaime and tells him that he will never see him again. Desperately, Jaime reaches his hand up and tearfully asks for his hand, grasping it, and then pleading with him not to go as the camera focuses in on their clasped hands.

At this point the shot is cut and a new take begins of the same scene, but this time with the grown Alejandro Jodorowsky entering the scene, and grabbing the hands of his sons, his actors. "No," he says, "not like this. Like this," he adds, raising Jaime from the dock so that he and young Alejandro now stands face to face in front of him. He pushes them together, and they embrace. He then addresses Adán (playing the young Alejandro) and tells him, with obvious anguish in his voice, "You went to France and never saw him again. When he died, you didn't shed a tear, but beneath your indifference, your heart was saying ... " He then stops narrating, and Adán takes up the words: "My father, by giving me nothing, you gave me everything. By not loving me, you taught me that love is an absolute necessity. By denying God, you taught me to value life," at which point Jodorowsky joins back in to say, "I forgive you, Jaime." He then hands Adán a pair of clippers and has him shave Brontis's head and mustache off. Brontis now shorn of the Stalin-like appearance he cultivated, smiles at young Alejandro, and the two kiss tenderly, the son thanking the father, the father blessing the son.

Young Alejandro then takes his leave on the same purple boat that ferried his family to Santiago at the end of *Dance of Reality*, this time alone with the skeleton, from whose back have sprouted white wings, while his parents and his memories, again, black and white cutout images from the film, bid him farewell from the dock. The voice over gives us one more poem, read by the real Jodorowsky, who intones:

I have learned to be.
I have learned to love.
I have learned to create.
I have learned to live.
Every path is my path.
Opening my heart,
I hear the woes of the world.[18]

In these dual endings, Jodorowsky has effectuated something like the end to an analysis, this one of himself. And as is well known in Lacanian analysis, ending an analysis essentially means one has become an analyst oneself, open and ready to hear the woes of the world.[19] The path Jodorowsky took there was his own, no doubt. And yet the steps are resoundingly similar. He engaged with a series of people and practices that he placed in the position of subject-supposed-to-know—teachers, yes, but also other artists, poets, lovers, and finally poetry and surrealism itself. Projecting into that transference a trust in the ultimate meaning that the Other had in store for him, Jodorowsky came to the realization that the subject-supposed-to-know in fact knew nothing. That it was on him and him alone to give birth to his authentic self.

What the final scenes in his last two films reveal is the subjective destitution that allowed Jodorowsky to cure himself, and ultimately set him on the path to becoming someone capable of curing others as well. Going back in his memory to the moment he left his family behind, never to see his father again, never to weep over his death, Jodorowsky staged a psychomagical action for himself, one in which he could relive that moment, and one allowing him to pierce the fundamental fantasy structuring the violence of his own desires: that whatever suffering still plagued him was the fault of his father, that his father in some sense, still existed, that Jodorowsky's work and efforts and desires were still unconsciously intended as a plea for his love, his admiration.

The dialogue that ends *Endless Poetry* is a repudiation of that belief. By forgiving his father but also reshooting the moment from his memory, with his sons, Jodorowsky also claims responsibility for his own path by saying every path is my own path, no one else but me has put me on this path. His father's neglect is transformed into a new birth: "by giving me nothing, you gave me everything. By not loving me, you taught me that love is an absolute necessity. By denying God, you taught me to value life." In a word, in the final scene of his final film, Jodorowsky has given us a version of what Lacan called moving from desire, where one's object is always mediated by some Other, to drive, an embrace of autonomy, of autochthony, of the contingencies that determine one's paths, and a willingness and ability to remain open to the pain of others, from wherever they may come.

NOTES

Chapter 1

1   Samuels, *Midnight.*

2   Jodorowsky, *Psychomagic,* my translation.

3   Freud, *Vorlesung,* 431–5.

4   See Derrida, "Plato's Pharmacy" and Žižek, "The Hair."

5   See Lacan, *Seminar III,* 179.

6   Jodorowsky, *Psychomagic,* my translation.

7   Jodorowsky, *Poesía sin fin,* my translation.

8   Žižek, "Hair," 72.

9   Lacan, *Four,* 225.

10   Lacan, *Four,* 225.

11   Lacan, *Four,* 232.

12   Žižek, "Hair," 72.

13   Jodorowsky, *Psychomagic,* my translation.

Chapter 2

1   Jodorowsky, *Fando y Lis.*

2   Augustine, *Confessions,* 244.

3   Plato, *Symposium.*

4   Egginton, "The Psychosis of Power."

NOTES

5   Lacan, "Instance," 417.

6   Lacan, "Instance," 422.

7   Freud, "Beyond," 599–601.

8   *Cheers*, Season 1, episode 5.

9   Carlin, *Back in Town*, 1996.

10   Lacan, "Signification."

11   Kant's full exposition of the antinomies can be found in Kant, *Critique of Pure Reason*, 459–551.

12   See Joan Copjec's "Sex and the Euthanasia of Reason," which maps the mathematical antinomies onto the feminine position and the dynamic antinomies onto the masculine position, and thus suggests that Kant was (unwittingly) the first theorist of sexual difference. The argument I make here differs somewhat, but in both cases the relation of Lacan's theory of sexuation to Kant's antinomies is central.

13   Nietzsche, *The Will to Power*, 481.

14   As Butler asks, "to what extent do the regulatory practices of gender formation and division constitute identity, the internal coherence of the subject, indeed, the self-identical status of the person? To what extent is 'identity' a normative ideal rather than a descriptive feature of experience?" *Gender Trouble*, 16.

15   Paul, "The Far Left."

16   Paul, "The Far Left."

17   Wittgenstein, *Philosophical Investigations*, 25 (investigation 50).

18   Of course by the same logic the Man doesn't exist, a point that merits less consideration simply because, believing implicitly they know what man, mankind, or men are, cultures tend not to bother themselves with the question.

19   Mitchell, *Psychoanalysis*, 402.

20   Žižek, *Sublime*, 112.

21   Nilsson, *When Darkness Falls*.

22   Castillo and Egginton, *What Would Cervantes Do?*

NOTES

23 Chiesa, *Subjectivity,* 149.

24 Žižek, "Hair," 76; Lacan, *Seminar X, passim.*

25 Precisely Kristeva's notion of the abject. See *Powers of Horror, passim.*

26 Ramis, *Analyze.*

27 Lynch, *Twin.*

28 Kael, Review of *El Topo.*

29 Jodorowsky, *El Topo.*

30 Freud, *Totem, passim.*

31 Brooks, "Why Mass Shooters Do the Evil They Do."

32 Quoted in 5Harfliler, "Healer, Rapist, and Cult."

33 Jones, "Why *The Holy Mountain* Is the Best Surreal Film Ever."

34 Girard, *The Scapegoat.*

35 We should keep in mind, however, that this literal castration is almost diametrically opposed to the concept's meaning in analytic theory.

36 Hobbes, *Leviathan,* 107.

37 Arendt, *Eichmann in Jerusalem.*

38 Jodorowsky, *Danza.*

39 Jodorowsky, *Santa.*

40 Lacan, *Seminar III,* 86.

41 More clinically minded theorists like Bruce Fink believe that if the paternal metaphor isn't instated by a certain age (usually around five or six), then the best that can be done for someone whose symbolic order lacks the paternal metaphor is to help them prop it up so as to minimize the likelihood of a psychotic break. As Fink puts it in his *Clinical Introduction to Lacanian Psychoanalysis:* "The symbolic order, missing a crucial element (the Name-of-the-Father), cannot be structurally repaired, to the best of our knowledge; it can, however, be propped up or 'supplemented' (to use Lacan's term) by another order" (101).

42 Phillips, "The Antihero's Last Gasp."

Chapter 3

1   Gibney, *How to Change Your Mind*.

2   Lacan, "Function," 208.

3   In fact, in his seminar Lacan also criticized the very notion of countertransference, which implies something different, illegitimate, as opposed to what Lacan believes is always the case in a conversation between two unconsciouses, as he defines the analytic situation. What others call countertransference, then, "is nothing other than an irreducible effect of the situation of the transference." *Le séminaire VIII*, 229, my translation.

4   Lacan, *Four*, 225.

5   See Laplanche and Pontalis, "Fantasy and the Origins of Sexuality," passim.

6   Apollon, "Psychanalyse et traitement des psychotiques," 88.

7   "Vous avez vu, en 68, vos structures. [...] Ce sont les gens qui étaient dans la rue !" Lacan apparently responded, "S'il y a quelque chose que démontrent les événements de Mai, c'est précisément la descente dans la rue des structures!" If the events of May show anything, it is precisely the taking to the street of structures. Dosse, 147.

8   Deleuze and Guattari, *Anti-Oedipus*, 108.

9   Álvares, "L'impromptu de Vincennes."

10   For what follows, see Lacan, *Seminar XVII* and Mark Bracher, *Lacanian Theory of Discourse*, passim.

11   Lacan, *Le séminaire XVII*, 34.

12   The following explanation borrows liberally from my book *How the World Became a Stage*, chapter 1.

13   Lacan, *Four*, 144.

14   Lacan, "Instance of the Letter," 430. This is the case despite what Lacan says at the beginning of the mirror stage essay, that everything in his thought goes against the idea of the Cogito ("Mirror Stage," 75). Of course, if we take the ego to be the same as the subject, as Descartes may be read as doing in his famous *ego cogito ergo ego sum*, then Lacan's thought does indeed run against the Cogito. But as subsequent interpreters have also

NOTES 169

underlined, once we understand the subject in Descartes to reside in the very split between the being of the sum and the being of the Cogito, then Lacan's subject does indeed become Cartesian. See, for instance, Dolar, "The Cogito as the Subject of the Unconscious."

15 Lacan, *Seminar I,* 42.

16 Jodorowsky, *Dance,* 41.

17 Jodorowsky, *Dance,* 41.

18 Jodorowsky, *Dance,* 2.

19 Jodorowsky, *Dance,* 2.

20 Lacan, "Function," 245.

21 Jodorowsky, *Dance,* 42.

22 Jodorowsky, *Dance,* 116.

23 Jodorowsky, *Dance,* 117.

24 Jodorowsky, *Dance,* 121.

25 Breton, *Nadja,* 160.

26 Jodorowsky, *Dance,* 85.

27 Lacan, *Seminar VII,* 321.

28 Jodorowsky, *Psychomagic.*

29 Jodorowsky, *Dance,* 137.

30 Seminar VIII, especially the introduction and section I.

31 https://www.rogerebert.com/reviews/great-movie-santa-sangre-1989.

32 https://www.rottentomatoes.com/m/santa_sangre.

33 The fact that Fenix sees himself as his mother's hands and hence everything he does as being done for her suggests that his fundamental psychic structure is that of perversion rather than psychosis, the basic attitude of the pervert being disavowal of the Other's lack. However, whereas those with perverse structures express that disavowal unconsciously by enjoying *for* the Other, psychotics fully and consciously believe that the Other is not lacking and experience that plenitude with an absolute certainty that stems from having foreclosed the substitutive function of the paternal metaphor.

Chapter 4

1   Jodorowsky, *Fando.*

2   Žižek, *Metastases,* 170.

3   Žižek, "From Desire."

4   Žižek, "From Desire." See also *The Ticklish Subject,* where he writes that normality is really just a more mediated form of madness. Žižek, *Ticklish,* 35.

5   Žižek, "From Desire."

6   Žižek, "From Desire."

7   Lacan, *Four,* 255.

8   Lacan, *Four,* 268.

9   Žižek, "Hair," 77.

10   Jodorowsky, *Dance,* 311.

11   Jodorowsky, *Dance,* 308.

12   Jodorowsky, *Dance,* 316.

13   Jodorowsky, *Dance,* 316.

14   Žižek, "From Desire."

15   Žižek, "From Desire."

16   Žižek, "From Desire."

17   Jodorowsky, *Danza,* my translation.

18   Jodorowsky, *Poesía,* my translation.

19   As of this writing, at ninety-four years of age, Jodorowsky has just announced on social media that he will begin work on the next film in his autobiographical series, *Viaje esencial.*

BIBLIOGRAPHY

5Harfliler, "Healer, Rapist, and Cult." November 2, 2021, https://www.5harfliler.com/healer-rapist-and-cult/

Álvares, Christine. "L'impromptu de Vincennes: Lacan et le discours *unis-vers-cythère* au lendemain de mai 68." Carnets, 2019, https://journals.openedition.org/carnets/9717

Apollon, Willy. "Psychanalyse et traitement des psychotiques." In *Traiter la psychose*. Eds. W. Apollon, D. Bergeron, and L. Cantin. Quebec: Collections Noeud, GIFRIC, 1990, 77–110.

Arendt, Hannah. "Eichmann in Jerusalem: Adolf Eichmann and the Banality of Evil." *The New Yorker*, February 17, 1963, https://www.newyorker.com/magazine/1963/02/16/eichmann-in-jerusalem-i

Augustine. *Confessions*. Trans. and Ed. Carolyn Hammond. Cambridge, MA: Harvard University Press, 2014.

Bracher, Mark. "On the Psychological and Social Functions of Language: Lacan's Theory of the Four Discourses." In *Lacanian Theory* of Discourse. Eds. M. Bracher et al. New York: New York University Press, 1994, 107–28.

Breton, André. *Nadja*. Trans. Richard Howard. New York: Grove Press, 1960.

Brooks, David. "Why Mass Shooters Do the Evil They Do." *The New York Times*, July 7, 2022, https://www.nytimes.com/2022/07/07/opinion/mass-shooters-motive.html

Butler, Judith. G*ender Trouble: Feminism and the Subversion of Identity*. New York: Routledge, 1990.

Carlin, George. *Back in Town*. 1996.

Castillo, David, and William Egginton. *What Would Cervantes Do? Navigating Post-Truth with Spanish Baroque Literature*. Quebec: McGill-Queen's University Press, 2022.

Cheers. Television series.

Chiesa, Lorenzo. *Subjectivity and Otherness: A Philosophical Reading of Lacan*. Cambridge, MA: The MIT Press, 2007.

Copjec, Joan. *Read My Desire: Lacan Against the Historicists*. Cambridge/London: MIT Press, 1994.

Deleuze, Gilles, and Felix Guattari. *Anti-Oedipus*. Trans. Robert Hurley, Mark Seem, Helen R. Lane. Minneapolis: University of Minnesota Press, 1983.

BIBLIOGRAPHY

Derrida, Jacques. "Plato's Pharmacy." In *Dissemination*. Trans. Barbara Johnson. Chicago: University of Chicago Press, 1981, 63–171.

Dolar, Mladen. "The Cogito as the Subject of the Unconscious." In *Cogito and the Unconscious*. Ed. Slavoj Žižek. Durham: Duke University Press, 1998, 11–40.

Dosse, François. *Histoire du structuralisme. Tome II: Le chant du cygne. 1967 à nos jours*. Paris: La Découverte, 2012.

Egginton, William. *How the World Became a Stage*. Albany: State University of New York Press, 2003.

Egginton, William. "The Psychosis of Power: A Lacanian Reading of Roa Bastos's *I, The Supreme*." *Journal of Foreign Languages and Cultures* 5.2 (2021): 4–11.

Fink, Bruce. *Clinical Introduction to Lacanian Psychoanalysis: Theory and Technique*. Cambridge: Harvard University Press, 1999.

Freud, Sigmund. "Beyond the Pleasure Principle." In *The Freud Reader*. Ed. Peter Gay. New York: Norton, 1989, 594–625.

Freud, Sigmund. *Totem and Taboo*. Trans. James Strachey. New York: Norton, 1989.

Freud, Sigmund. *Vorlesung zur Einführung in die Psychoanalyse und neue Folge. Studien ausgabe*. Vol. I. S. Frankfurt: Fischer Verlag, 1994.

Gibney, Alex, dir. *How to Change Your Mind*. 2022.

Girard, René. *The Scapegoat*. Trans. Yvonne Freccero. Baltimore: Johns Hopkins University Press, 1989.

Hobbes, Thomas. *Leviathan*. New York: Macmillan, 1958.

Jodorowsky, Alejandro. *The Dance of Reality. A Psychomagical Autobiography*. Rochester, VT: Park Street Press, 2014.

Jodorowsky, Alejandro, dir. *El Topo*, 1970.

Jodorowsky, Alejandro, dir. *Fando y Lis*, 1968.

Jodorowsky, Alejandro, dir. *Poesía sin fin*, 2016.

Jodorowsky, Alejandro, dir. *Psychomagic: A Healing Art*, 2019.

Jodorowsky, Alejandro, dir. *Santa Sangre*. 1989.

Jones, Will. "Why *The Holy Mountain* Is the Best Surreal Film Ever." https://www.tasteofcinema.com/2017/10-reasons-why-the-holy-mountain-is-the-best-surreal-movie-ever/

Kael, Pauline. Review of *El Topo*, dir. Alejandro Jodorowsky. *The New Yorker*, November 20, 1971.

Kant, Immanuel. *Critique of Pure Reason*. Trans. Paul Guyer and Allen W. Wood. Cambridge: Cambridge University Press, 1998.

Kristeva, Julia. *The Powers of Horror: An Essay on Abjection*. Trans. Leon S. Roudiez. New York: Columbia University Press, 1982.

Lacan, Jacques. *The Four Fundamental Concepts of Psycho-Analysis*. Trans. Alan Sheridan. New York: Norton, 1977.

BIBLIOGRAPHY

Lacan, Jacques. "The Function and Field of Speech and Language in Psychoanalysis." In *Écrits*. Trans. Bruce Fink. New York: Norton, 2006, 197–268.

Lacan, Jacques. "The Instance of the Letter in the Unconscious, or Reason since Freud." In *Écrits*, Trans. Bruce Fink. New York: Norton, 2006, 412–44.

Lacan, Jacques. "The Mirror Stage as Formative of the *I* Function as Revealed in Psychoanalysis." In *Écrits*. Trans. Bruce Fink. New York: Norton, 2006, 75–81.

Lacan, Jacques. *The Seminar of Jacques Lacan Book I: Freud's Papers on Technique*. Trans. John Forrester. New York: Norton, 1991.

Lacan, Jacques. *The Seminar of Jacques Lacan Book III: The Psychoses*. Trans. Russell Grigg. New York: Norton, 1993.

Lacan, Jacques. *The Seminar of Jacques Lacan Book VII: The Ethics of Psychoanalysis*. Trans. Dennis Porter. New York: Norton, 1992.

Lacan, Jacques. *Le Séminaire Livre VIII: Le transfer*. Paris: Seuil, 1991.

Lacan, Jacques. *Le Séminaire Livre X: L'angoisse*. Paris: Seuil, 2004.

Lacan, Jacques. *Le Séminaire Livre XVII: L'envers de la psychalanyse*. Paris: Seuil, 1991.

Lacan, Jacques. "The Signification of the Phallus." In *Écrits*. Trans. Bruce Fink. New York: Norton, 2006, 575–84.

Laplanche, Jean, and Jean-Bertrand Pontalis. "Fantasy and the Origins of Sexuality." *The International Journal of Psychoanalysis*, 49.1 (1968): 1–18.

Lynch, David, dir. *Twin Peaks: Fire Walk with Me*, 1992.

Mitchell, Juliet. *Psychoanalysis and Feminism: A Radical Reassessment of Freudian Psychoanalysis*. New York: Basic Books, 2000.

Nietzsche, Friedrich. *The Will to Power*. Trans. Walter Kaufmann and R. J. Hollingdale. New York: Random House, 1967.

Nilsson, Anders, dir. *When Darkness Falls*. 2006.

Paul, Pamela. "The Far Left and Far Right Agree on One Thing: Women Don't Count." *The New York Times*, July 3, 2022, https://www.nytimes.com/2022/07/03/opinion/the-far-right-and-far-left-agree-on-one-thing-women-dont-count.html

Phillips, Maya. "The Antihero's Last Gasp." *The New York Times*, July 20, 2022, https://www.nytimes.com/2022/07/20/arts/television/antiheroes-the-boys-batman.html

Plato. *Symposium*. Trans. Mary Louise Gill and Paul Ryan. In *Complete Works*, gen. ed. John Madison Cooper, Ed. D. S. Hutchinson. Indianapolis: Hackett, 1997.

Ramis, Harold, dir. *Analyze This!* 1999.

Samuels, Stuart, dir. *Midnight Movies: From the Margin to the Mainstream*, 2005.

BIBLIOGRAPHY

Wittgenstein, Ludwig. *Philosophical Investigations*. Trans. G. E. M. Anscombe. Englewood Cliffs: Prentice Hall, 1958.

Žižek, Slavoj, "From Desire to Drive: Why Lacan Is Not Lacaniano." *Atlántica de Las Artes* 14 (October, 1996), https://Žižek.livejournal.com/2266.html.

Žižek, Slavoj. "The Hair of a Dog That Bit You." In *Lacanian Theory of Discourse*. Ed. Mark Bracher. New York: New York University Press, 1994, 46–73.

Žižek, Slavoj. *The Metastases of Enjoyment*. London: Verso, 1994.

Žižek, Slavoj. *The Sublime Object of Ideology*. London: Verso, 1989.

Žižek, Slavoj. *The Ticklish Subject: The Absent Centre of Political Ontology*. London: Verso, 1999.

INDEX

1968. *See* protests

abjection 145, 167 n.25
acid. *See* drugs
agalma 146–7, 150, 155
allegory 55, 70
Althusser, Louis 17. *See also*
   interpellation
Analyze This! 40–1
anorexia 78
antiheroes. *See* heroes
antinomies. *See* Kant, Immanuel
anxiety 6, 36, 64, 73
Apollon, Willy 84
Arendt, Hannah 61–2
Arrabal, Fernando 12, 106. *See also*
   Fando y Lis
Augustine, Saint 13. *See also*
   Christianity
avant-garde 49, 82, 107–8, 112
Aztecs 54

Barenholtz, Ben 1
Benveniste, Émile 18–19. *See also*
   structural linguistics
bodies 1, 8, 11–12, 14, 21, 28, 37, 45,
   50, 52, 55–6, 61–3, 97–8, 119,
   123, 131–2, 135–7, 144–5, 147,
   160. *See also* castration; gender;
   mothers; paraplegia; sex
bourgeoisie 1, 53, 88, 138
Breton, André 18, 106–7
Brooks, David 47
Buddhism 31, 138. *See also* religion
Buñuel, Luis 51, 113, 147

burial 8, 42–3, 99–100, 115, 131–2,
   134, 156
Butler, Judith 26, 166 n.14

Cain, Michael 81
Cannes Film Festival 2
capitalism 92. *See also*
   commercialism
Carhart-Harris, Robin 77–8, 80
Carlin, George 20, 26
castration 11, 44–5, 56–9, 63–6, 69,
   71, 140, 142, 148, 167 n.35
Cheers 20
Chiesa, Lorenzo 36, 65
Chile 2, 65, 106, 108, 160–3
Chinese-Chilean community 108
Christianity 13, 52–5, 70, 123–4,
   132, 134–5, 137, 139–40, 146. *See*
   also conversion; Eden; Eve; Paul,
   apostle; Psalms; religion
circuses and circus performers 12,
   62–4, 126, 135, 146, 156, 158
coffins. *See* burial
Cogito. *See* Descartes, René
commercialism 54–5. *See also*
   capitalism
communism. *See* Marxism; Stalin,
   Joseph, and Stalinism
communities. *See* society and social
   relations
conversion disorder. *See* hysteria
conversion 100, 139, 141. *See also*
   religion
Copjec, Joan 166 n.12
corruption 54–5

176 INDEX

Crystal, Billy 40
cult film 1
cults 56, 59–61, 63, 75, 87, 94, 128.
    See also religion

Dalí, Salvador 5, 51, 113
Dance of Reality, The 2, 69–70,
    158–61, 163–4
Dark Knight, the 72
De Niro, Robert 40
de Palma, Brian 81
deafness 105, 126–7, 153
death 5, 36, 44, 53, 66, 114, 120–3,
    129, 131–2, 138–9, 164. *See also*
    femicide; honor and honor
    killings
Deleuze, Gilles 88
depression 6, 8, 73, 83, 100, 110–12
Derrida, Jacques 26
Descartes, René 7, 168–9 n.14
desire 4, 6–9, 12–14, 18, 20–7,
    29–33, 35–42, 47–50, 53–5,
    60–2, 65, 67–8, 70–5, 80, 83, 85–7,
    94–6, 98–9, 102–3, 105, 109–10,
    116–18, 120, 133–5, 139–43,
    147–8, 150–8, 160–1, 164. *See also*
    Lacan, Jacques
dictatorships. *See* totalitarianism
Disney studio 35
Down's syndrome 67
dreams 5, 16, 42, 58, 79, 83, 118,
    144
drive 8, 12, 15, 45, 55, 98–9, 103,
    140–3, 150–2, 154, 164
drugs 43, 46, 77, 138, 152
Dune 2

Ebert, Robert 126
Eden 6, 42, 71, 134
education. *See* gurus; teaching and
    teacher figures
Egginton, William 15, 34

ego 55, 74, 78–80, 82, 86, 92,
    96–7, 125, 132–3, 136–7, 140,
    142, 144–5, 147, 150, 161,
    168 n.14. *See also* identity and
    identification
Eichmann, Adolf 61–2. *See also*
    Nazism
Elgin Theatre 1, 46
Endless Poetry 2, 6, 69–70, 99, 103–4,
    106, 159, 161–4
Eve 42, 132. *See also* Christianity
existence 4–9, 20, 22–5, 30, 32, 38,
    64–5, 68, 71, 73–4, 76, 109, 133,
    145, 150–5, 153

Fando y Lis 11–12, 38–42, 70,
    116–18, 131–5, 140
fathers 8, 12, 22, 34–5, 44–5, 53,
    55–6, 65–7, 69, 71, 85, 111, 115,
    126–8, 153–4, 167 n.41, 169 n.33.
    See also gender; Jodorowsky
    Groismann, Jaime; parents;
    patriarchy
feces 125, 146–7
femicide 34–5, 41, 42, 63, 66, 68–9,
    126, 134, 156. *See also* gender;
    honor and honor killings;
    misogyny; *Santa Sangre*
feminism 29, 32. *See also* gender;
    misogyny
Fink, Bruce 167 n.41
France 1, 39, 88, 98, 106, 162. *See also*
    Paris
French language 30, 43, 95–6, 98,
    162
Freud, Anna 78
Freud, Sigmund, and Freudian
    theory 3, 16, 18, 21–2, 35, 44–5,
    52, 78, 82, 84, 88, 95, 98, 136, 142,
    144
functional neurological symptom
    disorder. *See* hysteria

INDEX

García Lorca, Federico 100, 103, 107
gender 17, 21–32, 34, 37–8, 41–5,
  47, 49–50, 67, 70–5, 109–10, 127,
  131–3, 135, 166 n.12, 166 n.14.
  See also femicide; feminism;
  homosexuality and homophobia;
  Identity and identification;
  intersexuality; misogyny;
  patriarchy; phalluses and the
  phallic function; sex; transgender
  people
Girard, René 52, 134. *See also*
  scapegoat
Goldman, Lucian 88
Goya, Francisco 16
graves. *See* burial
Guattari, Félix 88
gurus 7, 47, 75–6, 87, 89, 146, 149.
  See also religion; teachers

hallucinations 6, 15, 66, 68–9, 138,
  152, 154–7. *See also* drugs;
  psychosis; *Santa Sangre*
Harley Quinn, character 73
Harris, Eric 46
Hartmann, Heinz 78
Hegel, Georg Wilhelm Friedrich 44,
  122, 144–6, 148
heroes 46, 57, 72–3
heteronormativity. *See* gender
Hitchcock, Alfred 2, 11, 62, 67, 154
Hitler, Adolf 61. *See also* Nazism
Hobbes, Thomas 59.
Holy Mountain, The 2, 11–12, 45,
  51–8, 62, 70, 113, 124–5, 146–9,
  152
Homer. *See Odyssey, The*
homosexuality and homophobia 50,
  74, 100, 103, 162. *See also* gender;
  queerness
honor and honor killings 34–5, 40,
  134. *See also* femicide

horror films 36, 40, 65, 126, 155
hypnosis 3
hysteria 37, 89, 93–4, 127

Ibáñez del Campo, Carlos 158–60
identity and identification 5, 12,
  14–17, 22–3, 29–32, 34, 37–8,
  43–5, 71, 76–8, 80, 83, 85–7,
  90–1, 96–7, 102, 109–10, 125, 131,
  146–8, 151, 158, 161, 166 n.14.
  See also ego; gender
International Psychoanalytic
  Association 79
interpellation 17, 108, 118
intersexuality 26. *See also* gender
Ionesco, Eugène 113
Irons, Jeremy 35

Jackson, Ketanji Onyika Brown 28–9
jealousy 41
Jesus. *See* Christianity
Jodorowksy, Brontis 161–3
Jodorowsky Groismann, Jaime
  62–5, 100, 103–4, 107–8, 112–13,
  158–9, 161–4
Jodorowsky, Adán 162–3
Jodorowsky, Alejandro psychomagic
  and therapeutic practices of
  2–9, 49–50, 55, 70, 74–5, 87,
  99, 109–17, 133, 138, 140,
  149–50, 152, 164; surrealism and
  anti-surrealism of 2, 4–5, 12,
  42–4, 51, 56, 62, 104, 106–8, 112,
  117–18, 126, 133, 147; theatrical
  production and theatricality of, 1,
  3, 12, 39, 43, 50, 58, 99, 149; youth
  and education of, 1, 11, 64–5,
  99–104, 106–9, 136, 160–3. *See
  also individual films and passim*
Jones, Jessica, character 73
Jung, Carl, and Jungian analysis 50,
  58

178 INDEX

Kael, Pauline 43, 46
Kant, Immanuel 16, 23–5, 30–1,
    61–2, 76, 109, 166 nn.11–12
Klebold, Dylan 46
Klein, Allen 2, 51
Kreutzer, Marie 38
Kristeva, Julia 167 n.25. *See also*
    abjection
Krieps, Vicky 38

Lacan, Jacques 4–7, 16, 22–4,
    29–30, 39, 41, 45, 64–7, 75, 78–83,
    87–8, 110, 117, 120, 127, 146, 151,
    166 n.12, 168 n.7; psychoanalytic
    thought and legacy of, 6–9,
    30, 37–8, 50–1, 76, 79–81, 89,
    95–8, 128, 132–3, 140–4, 146–9,
    163–4, 167 n.41, 168 n.3, 168–9
    n.14; relationship to surrealism,
    4, 18; theory of discourse, 7,
    37–8, 89–95, 139; theory of
    language of, 4, 13–14, 16–20,
    23, 32, 102, 140, 142–4, 150. *See
    also* desire; gender; language;
    objet petit a; phalluses and the
    phallic function; psychoanalysis;
    quilting points; sex; surrealism;
    transference; *and passim.*
language 4–5, 20–1, 26–7, 32–3, 38,
    43, 70, 98, 102–5, 140, 143–4.
    See also Lacan, Jacques theory of
    language of; poetry; structural
    linguistics; writing
Lautréamont, Comte de 18
leftist thought and practice 27–9, 91,
    159. *See also individual figures
    and philosophies*
Lennon, John 1, 51
Lihn, Enrique 6, 105–6
Lion King, The 35–6
Lorenzio, Mara 48–9, 51
Lynch, David 2, 42–3.

Marinetti, Filippo Tommaso 107–8
Mars 57
Marxism 61. *See also* Stalin, Joseph,
    and Stalinism
mass murder 45–6, 48, 57–8, 61, 138.
    See also individual figures
masters. *See* gurus; teaching and
    teacher figures
Matrix, The 46
McGowan, Todd 42
menstruation 28
metric system 30
Mexico and Mexican people 51, 54,
    58, 61–2, 74
Miller, Frank 72
mime 1, 39, 126–7, 153, 157
misogyny 22, 34, 40–2, 49, 107,
    133–4. *See also* femicide; gender;
    patriarchy
Mitchell, Juliette 32
*Montaña sagrada, La. See Holy
    Mountain, The*
mothers 3–5, 12, 14, 16–17, 21–3, 32,
    42–3, 48, 63, 66–9, 85, 111–12,
    115–16, 119, 121, 126–7, 131, 143,
    153–7, 169 n.33. *See also* gender;
    parents; patriarchy; Prullansky
    Arcavi, Sara Felicidad

nationalism 35, 91
Nazism 61–2, 158–9
Neo-Platonism 13. *See also* Plato
Neptune 57–8
neuroscience 37, 77–9
neurosis 15, 37. *See also*
    psychoanalysis
New York 1
New Yorker, The 43, 61
Nietzsche, Friedrich 26
Nilsson, Anders 34–5
Nolan, Christopher 72
NXIVM 59–61

INDEX

O'Toole, Peter 2
objet petit a 15, 32, 35–7, 65, 84, 86, 89–92, 141, 147. *See also* Lacan, Jacques
obsession and obsessive-compulsive disorder 37–8, 71–2, 94. *See also* psychoanalysis
Odyssey, The 57–8
Oedipal complex 88
Ono, Yoko 1, 51
opera 108–9, 112, 159

Panic theater troupe. *See* Jodorowsky, Alejandro theatrical production of
pantomime. *See* mime
paranoia 15, 154
paraplegia 39, 53, 63, 68. *See also* bodies
parents 64, 82, 84–5, 100, 107, 111–14, 127, 152, 157–8, 160, 163. *See also* fathers; mothers; patriarchy
Paris 5, 30, 88, 93, 106, 115. *See also* France
Parmenides 13. *See also* Plato
paternal metaphor. *See* fathers
patriarchy 22, 24–5, 27, 31–2, 34, 40–2, 50–1, 66, 70–1, 73–5. *See also* fathers; gender; misogyny
Paul, apostle 100
Paul, Pamela 28–9
perversion 37, 71, 154, 169 n.33. *See also* psychoanalysis
phalluses and the phallic function 22, 24–5, 31–2, 45, 48–50, 64–5, 70–2, 74, 109–10, 128. *See also* gender; Lacan, Jacques
Phillip, Maya 72–3
phobia 74, 91
Plato 4, 13, 41, 146
poetry 1, 18, 75, 99–108, 126, 161–3
Pollan, Michael 77

pornography 28–9
pre-Socratic thought 13
protests 49, 56, 58, 61, 88–9, 93, 138. *See also* Thích Quảng Đức
Proteus 57–8
Prullansky Arcavi, Sara Felicidad 64, 99–100, 107–9, 112–13, 159–60, 164
Psalms 137, 139, 157–8. *See also* Christianity
Psycho. See Hitchcock, Alfred
psychoanalysis 3–9, 22, 31–2, 37, 40–1, 55–6, 59, 74–5, 78–89, 94–8, 117, 122, 127–8, 132–4, 140–1, 147, 149, 154–5, 159, 167 n.35, 167 n.41. *See also* ego; hysteria; Freud, Sigmund; Lacan, Jacques; transference
Psychomagic, A Healing Art 3, 5, 8–9, 49–50, 111, 115–16. *See also* Jodorowsky, Alejandro psychomagic and therapeutic practices of
psychosis 15–16, 62, 66–70, 147, 153–4, 167 n.41, 169 n.33. *See also* *Santa Sangre*
public life. *See* society and social relations
puppetry 1, 39, 68, 99

quadriplegia. *See* paraplegia
queerness 100, 103, 113. *See also* gender; homosexuality and homophobia
quilting points 33–5, 42, 103. *See also* Lacan, Jacques

Rainbow Thief, The 2
Raniere, Keith 59–61
rape. *See* sexual assault and slavery
reason 5, 16–17, 23–4, 30, 62, 92, 112, 144

rebirth 42, 49, 53, 71, 110–14, 129, 132, 135, 138, 151–2, 154, 164
religion 12, 34, 54, 62, 71, 75, 94, 99, 125, 128, 138–40. *See also* Buddhism; Christianity; conversion; cults; Eden; Eve; Psalms.
right-wing thought 28, 91. *See also individual figures and philosophies*
Romero, George 2.
Rotten Tomatoes 126

Santa Sangre 2, 12, 62–9, 125–8, 152–8, 169 n.33
Santiago. *See* Chile
Sarachu, César 35
Saussure, Ferdinand de 18, 102. *See also* structural linguistics
scapegoat 52–5, 134–5, 137
second-person expression 12
self-birth. *See* rebirth
self, sense of. *See* identity and identification
sex and sexual desire 5, 43–5, 47, 54–6, 67, 117, 126
sexism. *See* misogyny
sexual assault and slavery 39, 48–9, 51, 59, 115. *See also* femicide
sexual development and difference 5, 22–6, 30–2, 37–8, 41, 45, 50, 67, 70, 73–4, 91, 127, 133–4, 166 n.12. *See also* gender; patriarchy
Sharif, Omar 2
shit. *See* feces
signifier 4, 14–20, 32–4, 43, 89–92, 102–4, 127–8, 142. *See also* Lacan, Jacques; structural linguistics
silence 127–8, 153, 155–6. *See also* deafness; sound
Sisi, Empress of Austria 38
social media 42, 170 n.19

society and social relations 5, 15, 20–1, 29, 31, 48, 50–2, 71–3, 88, 98, 105, 110, 125, 133–4, 137, 145, 147, 150
Socrates 14, 146. *See also* Plato
sound 11, 18–19, 51, 56–7, 95, 97, 101, 107, 121, 135, 153. *See also* silence
Spain 8, 34–5, 54
Spanish language 27–8, 101, 126
speech act theory 20
staging. *See* theatre and staging
Stalin, Joseph, and Stalinism 158–60. *See also* Marxism
Stewart, Potter 28
structural linguistics 16–18, 88. *See also* Lacan, Jacques
superheroes. *See* heroes
Supreme Court of the US 28–9
surrealism 4, 6, 11, 16–18, 42–4, 51, 103, 106–8, 112–13, 144, 149, 163. *See also* Jodorowsky, Alejandro surrealism and anti-surrealism of
Symposium, The. See Plato

tarot 2, 53, 100–1, 125, 149
teaching and teacher figures 7, 47, 53, 75, 87–9, 92–4, 101, 103, 111, 119–24, 137, 139–40, 149, 163. *See also* gurus
television 42. *See also individual series*
theatre and staging 54, 82–3, 95–6, 99, 114, 117, 139, 160, 164. *See also* circuses and circus performers 12, 62–4, 126, 135, 146, 156, 158; Jodorowsky, Alejandro psychomagic and therapeutic practices of; Jodorowsky, Alejandro theatrical production of; mime; puppetry

INDEX

Thích Quảng Đức 138–9
Tlatelolco 58, 61. *See also* protests
Tocopilla. *See* Chile
Topo, El 1, 11, 43–9, 51–3, 55, 63–5, 70, 74, 109, 118–24, 134–5, 137–40, 152
totalitarianism 15, 88, 158–60. *See also* Nazism; *and individual figures*
transference 3–4, 6–8, 76, 80–7, 93–9, 104, 110, 115–19, 120, 124–5, 127–9, 133–4, 140, 146–7, 149, 152–3, 155, 160, 163, 168 n.3. *See also* Lacan, Jacques
transgender people 27–9, 113. *See also* gender
trauma 5, 36, 58–9, 63–8, 83–5, 114–15, 125, 131, 141–2, 151, 154, 161
Trump, Donald 91
Tusk 2

universities. *See* teaching and teacher figures

Viaje esencial 170 n.19
violence 1, 5, 27, 39–40, 43–8, 51–5, 58, 60–2, 65, 67–8, 70, 73, 75, 85–6, 109, 116–19, 126–7, 131–5, 138–40, 147, 152, 155–6, 161, 164

Waters, John 2
well-made play 82
western genre 11, 43, 46, 53
When Darkness Falls. See Nilsson, Anders
Wittgenstein, Ludwig 30
writing 4, 19, 101, 105, 108. *See also* poetry; theatre and staging; *and individual writers*

xenophobia 74, 91

Žižek, Slavoj 4, 33, 39, 97, 133, 140–3, 145, 150–2, 154–5, 170 n.4